Praise for "What Animals Tell Me"

Dr. Monica warmly relates her experiences of the healing power of communicating with animals after recovering her childhood telepathic connection. Walking us through her own skepticism of the information she receives, we learn about how animal communication works with her insights, confirmations, and results. Enjoy this compassionate addition to this amazing field.

—Penelope Smith, animal communicator and author of
Animal Talk and *When Animals Speak*

Through her captivating stories, Dr. Monica proves that animals can think and feel and that they experience lives not so different from our own. This courageous account of her psychic exploration will help you understand the power of your own mind and open your heart to the inner world of your animals. Bravo, Monica, on a job well done!

—Amelia Kinkade, author of *Straight from the Horse's Mouth:*
How to Talk to Animals and Get Answers

This book reveals animal thoughts, feelings, and motivations. When it is time to let your pet go, Dr. Monica's stories, advice, and wisdom will provide you with courage, compassion, and validation.

—Dan Poynter, author of *The Older Cat*

If you care, as I do, about your animals, this is one book you'll want to keep nearby. Learn that your animals are trying to communicate with you and how you can communicate back to them. You will be better able to care for your animals and help them live a better life.

—Jim Donovan, author of *Reclaim Your Life*

Your book is great. I enjoyed the many photos and stories. Like you, my favorite pastime is working with animals. They are so honest and so willing to communicate. The more books that are out on animals, the better it is. One of our missions on this earth is for people like us to teach as many people as we can how to communicate with animals and plants. We are doing just that. Keep up the good work.

—Patricia Murphy, author of *Cats/Canines Can Communicate*

I thoroughly enjoyed this book! Skeptics may scoff, but sooner or later animal communication will be recognized as a valid phenomenon. And when that happens, it will be thanks to books like *What Animals Tell Me*. Dr. Diedrich's humanity, modesty, and integrity shine forth on every heartwarming page. Three paws up!

—Helen Weaver, author of *The Daisy Sutra:*
Conversations with My Dog

What

Animals

Tell Me

About the Author

Monica Diedrich has heard animals speak since she was eight years old. By the age of eighteen, she was helping humans understand animals' feelings. Studying the Eastern traditions gave her an understanding of how nature, animals, and humans are interconnected, and how healing for all needs to be attained at three levels: mentally, physically, and emotionally.

Since 1990, she has been a pet communicator, talking to animals non-stop. She has also worked as a veterinary assistant. She holds a degree of Doctor of Metaphysics and is an ordained minister.

A native of Argentina, she has lived in Southern California for over thirty years with her husband and children (both human and companion animal).

Dr. Monica Diedrich

What Animals Tell Me

True Stories of an Animal Communicator

Llewellyn Publications
Saint Paul, Minnesota

FIRST EDITION
First Printing, 2005
Published in 2002 as *What Your Animals Tell Me* by Two Paws Up Press

Book design and editing by Rebecca Zins
Cover art © PhotoDisc, Inc.
Cover design by Lisa Novak
Interior posed animal images © PhotoDisc, Inc.
Interior candid animal photographs used courtesy of the author and her clients

Llewellyn is a registered trademark of Llewellyn Worldwide, Ltd.

Library of Congress Cataloging-in-Publication Data
Diedrich, Monica.
    What animals tell me: true stories of an animal communicator / Monica Diedrich.
    —1st ed.
      p.   cm.
    Rev. ed. of: What your animals tell me. 2002.
    Includes bibliographical references (p.   ).
    ISBN 0-7387-0629-9
      1. Pets—Behavior—Anecdotes. 2. Human-animal communication—Anecdotes. 3.
    Diedrich, Monica. I. Diedrich, Monica. What your animals tell me. II. Title.

SF412.5.D54 2005
636.088'7—dc22
                                                                    2004063241

Llewellyn Publications
A Division of Llewellyn Worldwide, Ltd.
P.O. Box 64383, Dept. 0-7387-0629-9
St. Paul, MN 55164-0383, U.S.A.
www.llewellyn.com

Printed in the United States of America

Contents

Photos

The photographs here are used by permission of the
animals and their companion people.

Preface to the Llewellyn Edition

Since this book first came out in 2002 (as *What Your Animals Tell Me*, published by Two Paws Up Press), it has been read by thousands of people. Hundreds have told me firsthand that, since reading the book, their perception of animals is completely new and meaningful.

Even my mother, who as a child was bitten by a large dog, can now walk by dogs she previously feared and smile, wondering about the kind of relationship they have with their human companions.

I have seen with my own eyes how a simple consultation changes the outlook of a person who comes in demanding some behavioral changes of their pet, only to leave with a new understanding of their companion animal—and of themselves.

Even skeptics or those who claim no particular affection toward animals have been affected by these stories. My Japanese translator, for instance, told me she dreams of a day when I can meet her in person so that I can teach her to communicate with pets. My Spanish translator told me that, after working on just half of my book, he went home to visit his mother, only to rekindle his relationship with the family dog, whom he now viewed in an entirely different way. Several of my editors now have a deeper understanding of their own pets after they have read, reviewed, and understood my words.

In particular, the chapter on names has surprised many people. I now find that more and more people are asking their pets if they like their names, which they are willing to change to make their pets happy.

Nothing makes me prouder than when people tell me they now have a much better understanding of their pets' needs and wants. They tell me that after reading this book, something has changed inside them.

Furthermore, the book has helped many people who realized that they, too, are capable of receiving information from their animals, but didn't understand how it was possible.

How wonderful it is that we are living in an age when we are no longer considered weird or crazy for communicating with animals! Now we are open minded, in tune with nature, and willing to learn; and, perhaps most importantly, we are willing to understand and ponder the lessons we receive from our companions.

I maintain that we are all able to communicate with other species. The fact that I was born this way only means that I had the ability to remember how it was done before languages existed; because of my sheltered life, it never became foreign to my soul. It was only hidden, waiting for the right time to emerge.

After you read the book for the stories, read it once more to understand the concepts. Animals do have feelings and emotions, likes and dislikes, and they do have souls. No, they are not humans, but their basic needs are similar to ours. We all need to understand one another so that we can live together harmoniously.

Even if you only find one thing here that resonates with you and your soul, my job will be complete. Then I could say that my journey on earth had a meaning and a reason for being—that whether I am still here or not, my voice remains in this book and hopefully in your hearts and minds.

Love always, unconditionally.

Dr. Monica Diedrich

Acknowledgments

This book did not come into being by itself. Along the way, I had many teachers, including the animals themselves, and many fascinating experiences and insights, which I share with you in this book. It really grew out of my simple intention of journaling my wonderful encounters with companion animals and, before I knew it, I had the beginnings of the book that is currently in your hands.

First and foremost, I must acknowledge the great teacher who helped me to understand myself and my gift and, by allowing me to be me, showed me how not to be afraid of the images I was seeing. Master Tam Nguyen accepted all my "pictures" with grace and understanding. He has always been my constant supporter because he believes in me.

Much later, I met Reverend Yvonne Goodale-Faber who, in her own way, guided me through being able to express my feelings and standing up for what I believed. She taught me about getting out of the boxes that society puts us in and opened me up to other possibilities.

Many other people who did not know they were my teachers but have greatly influenced me include Nick Babani, Nancy Allah, Lynn Licari, Nanette MacClellan, Susann Linn, Susan Payette, Shirley Dole, PK Odle, Darlene Mitcheltree, Dr. Allan Drusys, DVM, Annamae Crane, RVT, Tatyana Elmanovich, Isa de Quesada Gervais, Rick Streitfeld, Lydia Hibby, and all the people at the Association for Research in Metaphysics, my fellow ministers from the Metaphysical Fellowship Church, and the teachers and board of directors from the Learning Light Foundation.

Most of all, I want to thank my constant companion and friend of thirty-four years, my husband Albert, to whom I owe it all. His faith in what I do and his constant encouragement help me to do the very best I can. I could not have done it without his support.

The first edition of this book would not have come to fruition if it weren't for the great work by Tony Stubbs, who took me by the hand and guided me along the path. For this new printing, I want to acknowledge the wonderful team at Llewellyn who not only accepted my work out of hundreds of others but felt it was important to share.

And, finally, thanks to all the clients who called for consultations and who believed in my ability to contact their beloved animals. But mostly thanks to all the animals themselves who share their stories in these pages.

Introduction

"You do *what*?" people exclaim in amazement when I tell them I am an animal communicator.

"And how exactly do you do that?" they ask.

"Well," I reply, "I get pictures in my mind, like clips of a movie. These pictures tell me whether an animal is happy or sad, if it's longing for something or satisfied with its life. They show me their wants, desires, needs, and hurts."

The images I receive do not refer to time, so it may be hard to place the content of the picture in the past, present, or future. Also, the meaning depends greatly on the circumstances surrounding the event or the context of the situation. The images are often accompanied by impressions, feelings, tastes, sounds, and smells. I use all my senses when I am receiving the picture clips, so when I see a scene I also know how the animal feels about what I'm seeing.

Occasionally I call myself an animal behaviorist, which is tongue-in-cheek because most of the time any behavioral change called for is on the part of the human and not the pet.

People often assume that because I communicate with animals, I grew up close to them, observing them and sharing their lives. In fact, I grew up surrounded by apartment buildings in Buenos Aires, Argentina, a busy metropolitan city. The downtown area, where skyscrapers competed for the sky and for how many apartments or offices they could contain, was no place for pets. To see the slightest hint of green I had to walk to a park, the lungs of the city, a couple of miles away.

When I was eight, my family bought a summer home about two hours away from the city. It was a large Spanish-style home surrounded by lush greenery and lots of fruit trees. It was a little piece of heaven, away from the noise of taxi horns and exhaust fumes. All of my three-month-long school vacations were spent there and, on one such vacation, I realized that I could hear animals' thoughts.

On the corner next to us were neighbors who had emigrated from Europe. They had a farm and everyone within thirty miles knew the family and sought them out for fresh produce. They also kept chickens for eggs, cows for milk, a few work horses, a couple of dogs, and some barn cats. We felt lucky to have them nearby, as it meant that we would not starve, even during bad summer floods.

I would often go next door to buy milk and eggs. On one occasion, I was given a tour of the farm and saw a new mother pig with about twenty piglets beside her. I was surprised to hear her complain about how incredibly tiring she found nursing her young. As I "heard" this, she was looking right at me, and it was clear to me that I was not imagining it. I was paralyzed by this phenomenon and couldn't move for a long while. From then on, I volunteered to go for supplies all the time so that I could talk to the animals.

Once a dog tied to a tree told me how hot he was and laughed about the beating he received the previous day for breaking his chain. He said, "It didn't hurt that much—and besides, it was worth it. I got to inspect the whole ranch and marked everything. Now, even if I'm tied up most of the day, everyone will know it's all mine."

I also heard a cow that warmly offered me some freshly squeezed milk, and the chickens complaining about the new arrogant young cock.

At such a young age, I took these things for granted, never realizing that not everyone had this gift. Mentally, I simply replied to the animals and went on playing. It was not always pleasant, however. One day, a dog was about to be beaten and I clearly heard his desperate cry for help. The man undid his belt and called the dog to his side. The faithful animal, well aware of what was going to happen, obediently trotted over to him, shoulders slouching, head looking at the ground, and tail curled low between his legs. He looked at me and pleaded, "Tell him to stop, tell him not to do it."

"Please don't hurt him," I begged the owner, but to no avail.

"He needs to be taught a lesson," the man said gruffly.

Filled with anger and disbelief, I turned and walked away, the dog's cries ringing in my head. His pain was my pain. I ran home and vowed to never experience this again.

It wasn't until my eighteenth birthday that I realized I was different and began asking why I got extrasensory information from people and animals but others didn't. Why was vivid déjà vu an everyday occurrence? Why could I foretell events? For example, in conversations I routinely knew what someone would say next.

This was a matter of mild curiosity for me until the day my world stopped. I had just married and we went to a furniture store to buy furnishings for our new apartment. The moment I set foot in the store, I started to see a "movie" that showed me what the two-level store looked like, and I noted that the sweeping main staircase reminded me of the one in *Gone with the Wind*. I saw how every piece of furniture that we would buy was already in our new apartment. And I suddenly discovered why I was there and why this was happening. The picture inside my head showed me a little girl playing on the staircase accidentally falling and breaking several bones.

My mind raced. *What am I supposed to do?* I wondered. *Has this already happened? Or is it about to happen? And if so, what am I supposed to do? Stop the little girl? Tell her mother? Will someone tell me what to do,* I screamed internally.

The movie played for several minutes, during which time I actually saw a little girl begin to play on the staircase. She was jumping to the first step, then turning around and jumping to the ground. The next time, she jumped two steps and turned to jump back to ground level. She did this several times, each time jumping up one more step before turning and jumping down. I was motionless, watching and reliving my premonition. I counted six steps and, as I saw her begin to turn, I screamed. This startled her and she shifted her weight so that, unlike the premonition, when she fell she was only bruised, with no broken bones. She still cried and screamed for her mother, but I felt so relieved when I saw her stand up and run to her family.

Somehow my scream had changed the outcome. Shaken and confused, I wondered to whom I could speak about this. Who would understand? Would I be judged weird or, worse, insane? I decided to say nothing to anybody except God, the universe, or whoever out there was in charge and hopefully listening. "If I am never shown any bad things, then I will accept this gift and put it to work in helping people and animals. I will honor this promise as long as you never, ever show me scary things again."

Getting over the furniture store incident took many years. By then, however, I knew what the word "psychic" meant. I had read all the books by Jane Roberts in which she channels an entity named Seth, and was glad to learn that I wasn't the only one who was "strange." Jane Roberts had the same doubts that I had and as she recounted that she was, in fact, her own worst skeptic and critic, I began to feel more at ease. Then came other authors. And so my path began.

I wondered how to use my gift in a positive way to help animals. I reasoned that when you meet new people, you begin by asking them about themselves. So why not just do the same with animals? I will ask them questions and they will answer, I decided.

As I would come to find, animals are usually happy to describe their personality so that I can get to know them quickly. For example, they may describe themselves as "a little lady," "an old grouch," "an adventurer," or "a couch potato." Sometimes they explain their interaction with family members. They might tell me, for instance, that they are very close to Mom or Dad. (Most animals hold a parental-like image of their humans, so "Mom" or "Dad" often comes to mind.) Members of a multi-pet household talk about who is "top dog." A few talk about "friends" when describing the humans with whom they share a home. Amazingly, even those who are beaten and cursed talk lovingly about their families.

Some give me deep spiritual messages while others talk about their favorite food or activity. They all talk about love, about patience, and about having a job to do. Their jobs vary and are the most important part of their lives. Dogs, for instance, might take care of the house, watch for strangers, keep an eye on the kids, prohibit the cat from entering the room, or watch the baby. Outside dogs can go hunting, fishing, hiking, or herding. No matter what the job is, they always enjoy doing it well. They want to please their human companions and see them happy.

Cats, on the other hand, are more independent. Although some of them have a job, their main desire is to sleep, sunbathe, and do exactly what they want (as opposed to what you want). Still, they balance their wants and desires so that the relationship can be give-and-take. Granted, some of you give more than you take . . . or do you? At times, it seems as if our animals give us a lot more than we offer them. Their unconditional love is always there for us, regardless of how we treat them, and that far outweighs any payment or sacrifice that we can make.

Many of the stories in this book reveal that often our animals' main purpose is to teach us something about ourselves, and if they don't achieve that purpose in one lifetime, they will reincarnate back with us to continue their work. This may involve an animal getting the same sickness as its human guardian. With one of my clients, the animal died while the person made a complete recovery.

Understanding the role of our animals and what they do is sometimes far beyond our comprehension. By their actions, they mirror your feelings, showing you whether you're having a good day or a bad one. By being stressed themselves, they show you how stressed you are. Even when you show no outward signs of stress, they sense it because they can see your aura (the energy field surrounding your physical body) and become sponges, absorbing your stress for themselves. This helps you feel more relaxed. And what do you do then? You pet them and tell them you love them. They, in turn, show you their tummy, look at you with adoring eyes, or simply purr . . .

Purring signifies a magnificent feeling of contentment. To make your kitty purr with delight means that you must be a wonderful person. She needs you to show love, and you do. In return, she shows you just how special you are. After all, she doesn't purr for just anyone!

When our animals speak to us, they say things they need us to hear. They seldom complain, but they do want us to see their perspective. It's not enough for us just to understand what they're saying, though; often we must also take some action. If, during a consultation, I tell you that the reason your cat refuses to use her litter box is because it's dirty, I get concerned if you give me excuses such as, "I work long hours and get home tired," "I can't change the location of his box!" or "He always liked that brand of litter before." I can't change your animal's mind; I can only tell you what they tell me. It's up to you to act on it and do the changing.

Some people scoff when pet lovers ascribe human-like feelings to their animals. As an emotional empath, I disagree; every day, animals share their feelings with me. They can also rationalize what they want and what they prefer, including events and circumstances dealing with home and family.

It is my hope that this book will open a door in your mind. Even if you question my gift, please strive to be receptive to the insights it offers. Know that I have been as truthful and honest in every detail as I possibly can. Some of these consultations are on audio cassette for my reference, and others have been verified with the animal's guardian. The stories are all true!

Hopefully, this book will reveal the rich and deep inner world of our pets so that humans may appreciate them more. Animals know far more about what is happening in their lives—and yours—than we give them credit for. And, as you will see, they have souls that survive physical death, as do we, and often watch over us from the other side.

For clarification in the following accounts, I have put the animals' communications to me in quotation marks, as if they are speaking. Sometimes I do, in fact, hear actual words; when it is important, I get the whole sentence, and other times I get a few words with the movie clip. I hope this conveys the to-and-fro nature of our telepathic "conversations." So please relax and enjoy each chapter, filled with the animals' insights and perceptions, and walk alongside their families to experience how animals affect, enrich, and enlighten our lives every day.

CHAPTER 1

You Call Yourself a Healer . . . Do Something!

I am sitting on the floor of my bedroom watching my best friend die.

He has no control of his bodily functions and lies on the floor with eyes fixed on some imaginary object. His breathing is labored, his mouth open. My dog—my best friend, my "baby"—

might not make it through the night. My mind wanders back to the day we met. How tiny he was then! I chuckle at the thought of him quiet and secure inside my purse, occasionally sticking his head out as we go shopping. People would stop me to get a better look at the fluff of white fur that looked more like a chrysanthemum than a dog. When they realized they were looking into the bright, black eyes of a tiny puppy, they would tell me how beautiful he was. He eagerly soaked up their attention but always retreated to the comfort and safety of my arms. Today I can't even help him to feel good. He is dying before my eyes and I don't know what to do.

For many years, I had been studying the art of Cosmic Healing, a technique much like Reiki that is passed down from master to student. For the past twelve years, I had been guided by Master Tam Nguyen, my spiritual leader, in the fine art of channeling the healing energies of the universe to help people heal themselves. Every Saturday, I would go to the Association for Research in Metaphysics, in Anaheim, California, and spend many hours helping people with their problems.

Master Tam derived this technique by adapting it from Tantric Buddhism, and it is based on the heart chakra and the love of all things. It became a part of my life; when he asked me to be a teacher, I jumped at the opportunity.

Because of my fascination with Eastern thought, I studied Tibet—its culture, people, history and, of course, its pets—in particular, the Shih Tzu dog, known as the "lion dog from Tibet." The origin of the Shih Tzu breed is obscure. It is classified as a Chinese dog, since it was bred there for hundreds of years, but is considered to have originated in Tibet, where it was kept in the temples and occasionally given to the emperors of China as a tribute gift.

In Buddhism and its more mythical form, Lamaism, the lion is held as a sacred animal. The Buddha Manjusri, the god of learning, is said to have traveled the four continents as a simple priest, accompanied by a small dog. In an instant, the dog could transform into a mighty lion with Buddha riding on its back. The Tibetan Lamas probably encouraged breeding Shih Tzus to resemble their "lions," and undoubtedly their best specimens would have been selected. To be given a lion dog was a great honor, and the last tribute gift to the Chinese emperors was made in 1908, when the Dalai Lama, bringing several dogs, visited the Empress Dowager some months before her death.

The small lion dogs were kept for temple duties and as house pets, where they lived as members of the family. Following the death of the Empress Dowager Tzu Hsi in 1908, there was no one to supervise dog breeding in the Imperial Palace. The new emperor, Pu-Yi, was not interested in the palace dogs, so many of them were given away to important Chinese families and high-ranking foreign officials, while others were sold in the dog markets of the Lamaist temples.

Dog breeding continued outside the palace and it was believed that the Chinese would go to great lengths to prevent live dogs and puppies from leaving the country, including feeding powdered glass to exported dogs just before they left for the West.

With the Chinese invasion of Tibet, the breeding stopped and the dogs disappeared. Years later, some of them were found in Shanghai and sold to General and Mrs. Douglas Brownrigg, who fell in love with the breed. They took them to England in 1931 and, after many tries, successfully bred a couple of females. Shih Tzus were brought to the United States in 1966 and rapidly became one of America's favorite lap and toy dogs.

I became enchanted with the breed and its history, and set out to find one. After much research, I found someone who had been breeding them for many years. The trip took over an hour and I was filled with anticipation. I had been to two other kennels before but none of the puppies was what I was looking for. When we finally arrived, I was discouraged; they had only one puppy left, an eight-week-old male.

Even though I wanted a female, I took one long look at him with his white fluffy coat, curly tail, and big, black, expressive eyes, and fell in love. I was hooked.

He came from a long line of champions, both American and English. Wanting to keep his Chinese roots alive in him, I named him after one of his ancestors, Chop-Chop, meaning "fast," because he would run quickly to me when I called him. He was my first animal love.

Chop-Chop was a happy, sweet, obedient, and playful puppy, very close to the family and eager to please. He would always come when called and never had any "accidents" inside the house. The perfect gentleman never barked either.

One day when he was two years old, I was going upstairs to my bedroom and called out for Chop-Chop to follow me, as was customary, but he didn't come. My puzzlement turned to alarm when he began to whine and looked up, then down. First I called out more loudly, then enticingly with a soft cooing voice. He just kept whimpering. I went back downstairs and picked him up. As soon as I put my hand around his belly, he let out a piercing yelp—an unmistakable cry of pain.

My children confirmed that he had been quiet all day, lying down most of the time. I was very concerned for him and settled him down with padded blankets for the evening. Once settled, he didn't complain and was asleep in minutes.

The next morning brought no improvement. He wouldn't follow me out to go potty and I had to lift him up from his bed and take him outside. He squatted like a female instead of lifting his leg. Again, not like him.

I immediately took him to the veterinarian, who diagnosed hip dysplasia compounded by a pinched nerve in his spine, worsened by the severe cold, humid weather we were experiencing. The doctor gave him a shot for the pain and prescribed medication to be given twice a day for ten days. He said there was no real cure and warned me to start

4

thinking about hip replacement surgery, even though that offered no guarantees. The only other option was euthanasia.

I was distraught. Chop-Chop was only two years old. He'd never shown any sign of this disease until now and he barely weighed twelve pounds. In my attempt to deal with the situation, I reasoned that the vet was wrong. Chop-Chop had probably just hurt himself playing with one of my boys. Surely the painkillers would make him feel better by tomorrow, I rationalized. They didn't.

As time passed, walking became progressively more difficult for him, until finally he was paralyzed from the waist down. He was in so much pain that he couldn't even pull his body along with his front paws. What's more, he would lie still, eyes fixed on an unknown horizon, for hours at a time. He was no longer able to control his body functions, so I bought him diapers. All this happened in a matter of days.

I took him to another vet, who also diagnosed him with the same condition and prescribed more of the same ineffective pain medication. Chop-Chop would not eat and rarely drank. It became painfully clear to me that he did not have long to live.

I cried all the way home from the vet, and cried some more while telling my husband of this second visit. I cried even more at my own helplessness. That night, I put some warm blankets on the floor next to my bed and stared at Chop-Chop for the longest time. He wasn't staring back. He was lost again in that state of blankness where everything else makes more sense than where you are in the here and now.

Thinking that this might be his last night with me, I couldn't go to sleep so I grabbed my own blanket and laid down next to him on the floor, talking to him gently. Suddenly, a voice startled me: "Well, you call yourself a healer. You've helped a lot of people . . . *so do something!*"

I was shocked and sat up immediately to look around the room. Of course, I was alone with Chop-Chop. When I looked down at him, I realized that he was talking to me by mental telepathy. For the first time in days, he looked me directly in the eye and gave me a long stare.

Chop-Chop and Princess

Top: Chop-Chop rests his head on Princess Tatiana.
Bottom: Princess Tatiana, right, is the love of Chop-Chop's life.
They are now both senior dogs of thirteen years.

At that moment, the connection between us was so strong that I realized we were communicating on another level and he was putting his trust in me and my abilities to channel the healing light.

"Of course," I gasped. "Why didn't I think to apply Cosmic Healing to animals? It will work the same as it does for humans."

Quickly, I began to put all my knowledge, effort, and concentration into the task at hand. I invoked the cosmic energy, talked to the heavens, spirit, the universal light and love, the angels and fairies, my higher self and guardians, and all the saints and sages of all time, space, and dimensions. I asked everyone and everything that was, is, or will be to help me be the transmitter of life and healing light. I waited for a sign. My hands became very hot and the usual prickling sensation followed. I knew I was ready.

My hands were directed to start at the base of the neck, the beginning of his spine and, with a slow pulling and pressing motion, they traveled the length of his back until they reached the base of his tail. My mind thought to stop, but my hands kept on going as if they knew what to do. They grabbed his tail, which curves up and around, and pulled slightly, thus manipulating his whole spine. My hands then concentrated on the hip area and manipulated his legs into strange contortions. Finally my hands moved to his belly area, where the weak stomach muscles were making him bear the weight of his body. I watched different patterns emerge as I let my hands be guided to heal. Then the flow suddenly stopped. I thanked everyone and bowed my head in reverence and gratitude. My belief was unwavering that I was doing everything I could for his highest good. Satisfied with this, I slept soundly the whole night for the first time in days.

When I got out of bed the next morning, Chop-Chop got up on all four legs and shook his mane, something he had not been able to do for a long time. I was so happy to see him do that much that I immediately picked him up and took him outside to relieve himself. I was careful to put him down gently for fear that his back legs would give out on him,

7

but he stood firmly and relieved himself without difficulty—still squatting, however.

We went inside and I gave him another healing session. After our customary breakfast and sharing time, I went to work. When I came home that evening and took him outside again, he was able to stand much better, and I was pleased that the healing was indeed doing some good. I gave him another healing that evening. By the next morning, he was in good spirits and, when I took him outside, he slowly walked two or three feet until he found his spot and I could see him trying to lift his leg. Within a week, he was back to his normal self.

That was years ago, and the dysplasia has not recurred, nor has he had any other health problems. I believe that he volunteered his body to teach me an invaluable lesson—that universal healing energy is here to give hope, light, and healing for all living things; and that's exactly what I've been doing ever since.

Regardless of whether I offer healing or communication with pets, healing always happens in the session; healing of the heart and mind are just as important as physical healing. And when my clients call me because they need closure after a pet has died, the session is always healing.

I can offer my human clients nothing better than the opportunity to understand their companion animals. My gift to them is to let them know what animals like or dislike, and to glimpse their personalities and attitudes toward their life and family. They have something to say about everyone around them, be it human or animal, as in the first story.

Jonathan

One Saturday, I was having a garage sale at home when the phone rang. One of my clients was concerned about Jonathan, her eleven-year-old mini dachshund who was having a seizure in the middle of the living room. It was very hard to concentrate at that moment and leave behind what I was doing, but I did the best I could over the telephone. I asked Jonathan's mom to concentrate with me and we went through some guided visualizations designed to bring Jonathan back into balance. He kept sending me images of green pastures and a big tree so I asked her to take him to a park. "Take his favorite blanket and have him lie down in the shade for about an hour, and call me back later."

She called me later in the afternoon and thanked me profusely. "Jonathan is acting better than he has all month. I want to make an appointment to see you in person."

When they came in, we talked extensively about Jonathan's various concerns. Uppermost was his concern over his mom's plans to move to another state in the immediate future. This stressed him to the point of having chronic seizures. He needed some details that would make the change to another home a little smoother, which Mom and I gave him.

Not long after I saw him, I got a call from Mom telling me the seizures had stopped and they were both ready for their big move.

When I give a class or a workshop, I try to make sure that everyone understands "healing" as a principle of life. The Bible says that we all possess a "divine spark" inside of us. This divine spark is part of what we call God, or Universal Energy, the Tao, the All That Is, etc. It is what connects us to the universe and to each other. This sublime energy can be harnessed for the good of others. When we do good unto others without expecting anything in return, we get a lot more returned to us with the same good spirit. That's why, when I do good for the animals,

9

I get so much love in return that I have no doubt this is one of my missions in life.

Calling in a professional healer is not always practical, so at the end of this chapter, I present a healing technique you can perform yourself. All you need is love, good intentions, concentration, and imagination, as in the next story.

Shadow

I went to visit Shadow, a two-year-old Great Pyrenee, because Ann, her mom, was concerned that lately she had been acting strangely. "She doesn't enjoy visiting with people or places anymore, and starts whining and pawing at me because she wants to go home. I'm curious to know what's wrong."

A day or so before the session, I send the animal a message that I am going to be visiting for a "talk," so the animal knows in advance. I'd done this with Shadow so, when I arrived, she greeted me at the front door and immediately let me pet her. She felt at ease with me and I with her. We cuddled and she smelled my body and hair thoroughly. While I knelt down to talk to Shadow, Ann was amazed. "I can't believe it. Shadow always jumps up at people and then brings one of her toys to the guest for play."

When I explained, "Shadow was not about to do that with me," Ann was perplexed. "Shadow knows that I am here to 'talk' and not play," I added.

Ann, still amazed, asked, "Did you tell Shadow not to jump on you?"

I smiled and answered, "No, I didn't."

We talked for a while about Shadow's recent problems, about her separation anxiety, and about how she had destroyed her carpet and other things. Then she complained about pain in all four knees, but especially her right hind hip and knee areas. Ann explained that when Shadow had been a year old, she'd had surgery on her left knee. When

You Call Yourself a Healer . . . Do Something!

the conversation turned to her sleeping habits, Shadow complained, "I can't find the right place to lie down because I am experiencing some pain in my bones. Several times a night, I need to get up and try to find a comfortable place to lie down."

Next, Shadow sent me an image of her standing up on her hind legs playing with other dogs, as if wrestling. Ann verified, "That's exactly what Shadow likes to do when I take her to the leash-free park."

In view of Shadow's complaints, I was puzzled by the image until she explained that she was no longer able to play rough. I suggested to Ann that she take Shadow to her vet for a checkup. We talked about a few other things and I left Ann with a new understanding of her "big girl."

Ann called me less than a month later. "I took Shadow to the leash-free park for an afternoon of fun. She soon found a friend, a big German shepherd, she could play with. After a couple of minutes, though, she yelped really loudly and fell to the ground after being up on her hind legs. I rushed her to the vet, who said that she'd pulled her right kneecap off and needed immediate surgery. Shadow was right all along. It was her right leg."

Ann went on, "I'm concerned about the operation's success but I'm more worried about her recuperation. She's a big girl, about 150 pounds, and will be off her feet for a few weeks. Could you come see her again?"

When I got to the house, Shadow was waiting for me, standing on three legs and wagging her tail. She recognized me right away and limped over to the sofa and lay down. I could see that her right rear leg had been shaved. She had been opened from the upper thigh in a straight line down the front of her knee, almost to the ankle. Many staples held the wound together, which was a little swollen.

Shadow asked Ann many questions, starting with why she'd needed the operation, why there was so much pain, how long before the stitches would be removed, and how long before she could get out of confinement.

11

Shadow

This beautiful Great Pyrenee benefited from our healing sessions, even giving me a hug afterward.

Shadow complained about back pain because she was not used to distributing her substantial weight unevenly on three legs. She also complained about a noise coming from the outside. "The pounding is bothering me and won't let me rest."

Ann explained, "The rain is dripping down the chimney. Tell Shadow that if she wants, she can move to the living room."

Shadow replied, "Not now. I'm very tired."

I explained to Ann how to harness the light energy and do some hands-on healing by transmitting the energy with love into the body of Shadow while at the same time using her imagination. We did it together and I asked her to do it twice a day. I added, "Next time she goes to the doctor, he might tell you that she is healing faster than anticipated. That will be your cue that what you're doing is working."

Ann diligently used this technique on Shadow and, as I predicted, the doctors and nurses were surprised that Shadow was healing a lot faster than they expected.

Because so many people ask me what they can do to help their animals overcome surgery or injuries, I would like to share with you the following healing technique I introduced to Ann for Shadow. Please note, however, that this is not a substitute for veterinary care, but a supplement to it. If your animal is sick or injured, always consult a veterinarian.

The Healing Process

Sit quietly in front of your animal friend and close your eyes. Breathe in deeply three times while imagining that, with each breath, you are receiving the healing light of the universe through your nostrils. As you breathe, the energy accumulates in your lungs and then is transferred to your stomach. The Chinese Masters call this spot the *tan t'ien*, an area located approximately three inches below the navel and two and a half

13

inches inward. This is the center of your aura, the balancing area of your internal energy, your grounding point.

Continue with slow, rhythmic breathing and position your hands with palms up, elbows elevated, and fingers pointing outward, as if gesturing "Why?"

Continue breathing in energy until you feel a prickling sensation in your fingertips or heat in the palms of your hands. Sometimes the energy will come from the top of your head and travel down your body. Then turn your palms down, lightly touch the affected area, and direct the healing energy into your pet. No massage, no caress, just hands-on healing. Feel this healing warmth radiate through your body and into your pet's body. Know that, as this transfer is happening, you are only a channel for the light, much like a TV antenna. The energy is always around us; all you are doing is harnessing it and transferring it to where it is most needed.

While you're doing this with your hands, imagine that you are being helped by an army of little people. They are volunteers from the spirit world and are at your service for helping others. Think of *Gulliver's Travels,* when the whole town of Lilliput tried to tie up the huge monster asleep on their beach. That's exactly what I'd like you to picture, only in this case, the army of volunteers is armed with instruments made out of light. The first battalion has thread and needles made of light, and they will go over the sutures, sewing, so that the wound closes perfectly and heals rapidly. The second battalion is armed with sponges made out of light that, when pressed on the wound, make the light penetrate and heal faster. The third battalion has tiny syringes filled with love and light that, when injected into the muscles, will help them to grow, stretch, and be pliable once more. The fourth battalion reflects light with their shields into the immune system to reactivate it and, in so doing, allow the red blood cells to grow.

Maintain these images for as long as you can; usually ten to fifteen minutes will be sufficient. Once you can't hold the visualization any longer, let everyone go by thanking their efforts and releasing them until next time. Thank the divine spirit, the heavens, your god, the Tao, or whomever you believe in, and add that you are doing this for the highest good of all. Believe in this.

This is a great visualization technique that provides your mind with an avenue for doing something for your beloved pet instead of feeling helpless and doing nothing. It also helps your mind by concentrating on the task at hand and mentally exercising your focus for the end results you expect.

As always, meditation is a great tool and that is where everything begins. I encourage all my clients and students to start their road to a new awareness by meditating at least once a day, every day, at the same time and in the same place, for a period of at least ten minutes.

Meditation is nothing more than giving yourself a chance to listen to what your higher self needs to tell you. It is a non-doing, non-thought state of being where you are able to receive information from a higher source. One of the best ways of meditating is by breathing deeply and counting your breaths. Another is to concentrate on a single object such as a candle, the flames of a fireplace, a blade of grass, a flower petal, or the foam of a wave. You can meditate anywhere, anytime.

CHAPTER 2

What's In a Name?

When you name a living creature, you are, in effect, acknowledging certain qualities and vibrations that resonate with you. You might decide on the name of a person, a TV character or personality, a cartoon or a hero. They reflect how you view your pet or what qualities you like. Many times, people grow up with a name they absolutely hate and change it when they get to be adults; others like their name because it feels good to them. Perhaps a friend or family member gives us a nickname. We may become so familiar with it because it feels right that we go through life introducing ourselves by that name instead of our given name. American Indians followed a custom of naming their children after natural phenomena—qualities found in nature and animals (Running Brook, Swift Deer), events that occurred around the time of childbirth (Dark Storm Cloud), or the baby's appearance (Smiling Eyes).

Australian aborigines have an even better custom. Children are named at birth and, as they develop and outgrow their birth name, they choose a more appropriate name, possibly changing names several times in life as their wisdom, creativity, and sense of purpose grow.

For our pets, the situation is a little different. Usually they have no say in what we name them, and some of them do not like their given names. All I know is what your pets tell me, and they do talk about their names . . . a lot!

The Black Twins

One summer I consulted with the guardian of two male cats. They had different parents but were so much alike that they actually looked like twins: black, short hair and light green eyes. One of them was named Dingolin; the other, Little Shit.

As soon as I made contact with Little Shit, he told me, "I am very, very upset with such a disgusting name. I feel offended. I've always felt that Mom committed a terrible offense against me."

When I conveyed to him that Mom apologized, saying, "I always call you Little Baby instead," he told me that no amount of apologies could compensate for his hurt feelings. And neither did he find "Little Baby" funny at all. Anyway, I impressed upon his mom never, ever to refer to him as Little Shit. He was very serious about it!

Mom was really more concerned about Dingolin, who was dying of kidney failure. When Little Baby was done, he simply turned his head toward the window and stopped sending me any more information. He said only, "It's his turn now," so I turned to talk to his brother.

Dingolin had just returned from a three-day hospital stay. He wanted so much to live. He loved his home and his mom; like his brother, his name was the only thing he was unhappy with. Feeling so sick, he refused to drink water, and no promises of warm arms would entice him to come when called. He had retired to a spare bedroom and would hide for most of the day, as far away from his food and water as possible. Only when he needed some affection would he come out and stretch up as far as he could to touch his mom on her face with his right paw, thus telling her he was ready for some love.

I talked with his mom about her own kidney troubles, how our pets take on our diseases and mirror our feelings, and how, in the end, by taking care of ourselves and our own problems, we start taking care of them as well. She understood and instituted some changes right away. When I called three months later, both boys were doing well and enjoying their new names, Sweetie and Dini.

Sometimes we can be a little obsessive with the names we give our pets. I still do not understand the reason why one of my repeat clients names her pets after famous people. Her rabbits are named Sammy Davis, Jr., Dean Martin, and Joey Bishop; her two cats are Peter Lawford and Frank Sinatra (even though "Frank" is a girl). When I asked her about it, she said, "My husband and I are avid fans of the original Rat Pack."

As the next story shows, sometimes pets can be just as obsessive over their names as we are.

Amber

Jean shared her home with two beautiful female Himalayan cats. One was 1½-years old and named Beauty Emilia Huntress. She loved that name, and just to show her mom how correct she was when she named her, she used to run around hunting fuzzy toy mice.

The kitten, 5½ months old, was named Smokey Amber. When I approached Smokey, I realized that, although a beautiful seal point, her eyes were blue and not amber. I asked her mom, "Why did you name her Amber when she has blue eyes?"

She said, "Smokey was lying in front of me while I was experimenting with different names out loud. When I said 'Amber' she looked up, so I knew that she liked the name."

I was able to confirm that fact during our conversation. Jean had done everything right. She'd experimented with different names and waited for a reaction from her cat. But at the last minute, she had chosen a name that *she* liked. After our conversation, though, the cat's name was changed to Amber Smokey.

Amber

Lady

Even when a name seems perfect for a pet, the animal still might not like it, as was the case with one of my own. As a long-time Shih Tzu breeder, I find them to be exceptional with children, adults, and other animals, as well. They are lap dogs, they love to be petted and handled, and they are at their best being next to you.

When Chop-Chop was a year old, I bought a female Shih Tzu and named her Princess Tatiana (see page 6). She quickly became the love of his life, and still is. They act like a married couple; they sleep touching each other, go out together, climb on the sofas together, eat at the same time, and lick each other every day.

In one of their litters there was a little puppy that was smaller than the rest. Her colors—white and gold—were unusual for a Shih Tzu, so I decided to keep her and named her Lady Madonna, or Lady for short.

Two years later, I had three adults and eight puppies that were nearing their weaning period. We sent the word out to people we knew, and soon had a waiting list.

One day, out of the blue, Lady, now two years old, told me, "It's time for me to be special. I want to find a good family where I don't have to share the lap of my human with anyone else. I long to be the one and only."

I listened to her, my heart breaking, and promised to try to find her such a home. Well, to be honest, I didn't. I loved her too much and couldn't bear the thought of letting her go. How could I? I struggled with the idea of interviewing someone to be my little baby's new mom but, when I thought of placing an ad, all I could think of was the chilling phrase "Free to good home." What value can you place on two years of love and affection?

About this time, I had Lady spayed because she'd had her first litter of puppies and was proving to be a terrible mother. She wouldn't stand

21

still to feed her puppies, refused to clean them, and would disappear for hours while her mom, Princess, would have to clean up her grand-pups.

I put all thoughts of her leaving behind me, at least until the universe proved that it knew better than I what was in the best interest of everyone involved, human and animal. One day, a couple—Mr. and Mrs. Woodbridge—called, looking for a puppy. I told them that I had eight and invited them to visit.

When they arrived, I showed them the puppies and we spent half an hour talking about them and how to take care of them. Suddenly they asked me, "Could we see the older dog?" (My husband later told me that he'd mentioned Lady when they'd called for directions but had said nothing to me, thinking I would be angry with him.)

I was stunned. Barely able to think clearly, I asked, "Why do you want an older dog?"

Mr. Woodbridge explained, "I'm retired now and although I'm home most of the time, I don't think I have the stamina to raise a little puppy. About three months ago, we lost our little female Shih Tzu and we feel so lonely and the house is so empty that we want a young dog, one that will outlive us this time. We've been searching for months for a gold and white Shih Tzu and haven't been able to find one."

I agreed with them that the coloring was difficult to find. Unsure of my feelings and regretting every step, I went outside and had a "talk" with Lady. I told her, "There's a couple here who want to meet you. They might be the family you're looking for. But I can't and won't make a decision on your behalf. If you feel that they are the new family you're hoping for, you must let me know in no uncertain terms. It's the only way I'll let you go."

She agreed, so I picked her up to hug her and tell her how much I loved her, and brought her into the house. As soon as I put her on the living room floor, she happily started smelling them. She jumped on the couch to visit with the woman, and then jumped down and up to visit with the man on the other couch. For about five minutes, she went back and forth between them while I made idle conversation just to keep my mind occupied.

What Lady did next really shocked me. Sitting on the man's lap, she slowly, sheepishly, but purposefully licked his chin twice. Now, she'd never before licked people and certainly not faces, so this was highly unusual behavior for her. Next, she stared at me for what seemed an eternity, then looked up at him, gave him another lick, and curled up on his lap. (See chapter 3 for a deeper explanation of this uncharacteristic behavior.)

Youshie

The Shih Tzu formerly known as Lady.

I'd asked for an unmistakable sign that she approved of the couple, and had received it. With a broken heart, I agreed that they could take her on a one-week trial to make sure they all liked each other.

Mrs. Woodbridge asked me, "Do you think Lady would mind terribly if we gave her a new name?"

When I asked Lady, she told me, "I've never been too happy with that name and would love a new one."

When I conveyed this to Mrs. Woodbridge, she said, "We'll call her Youshie, after our first dog."

The new Youshie not only took to her name but also, before the week was over, had stolen the hearts of the two people whom she had picked as her new parents. She is, to this writing, an inseparable part of their lives, accompanying both of them everywhere, even into the morning shower!

Thank you, Youshie, for teaching me a great lesson in letting go. Thank you also for teaching me the importance of names. By allowing your new parents to give you a new name, you gave them an immediate sense of belonging that can only be surpassed by your love and affection.

Butch

"This is Naomi and her dog, Joey," my assistant announced. It was Saturday morning and I was consulting in a local animal training club's fundraising event that included Breed Conformation, Obedience Trials, and Canine Good Citizen certification.

Joey was a huge, five-year-old male Rottweiler who looked at me with intense eyes. As he sat down, he gave me a familiar smirk that made me believe that some dogs actually can smile! No sooner had I closed my eyes and made contact when Joey told me in no uncertain terms, "That is not my name! It's a sissy name and I will not respond to it in any way!"

Naomi was so surprised to hear how adamant her dog was about his name that she was speechless. I asked her, "What's his real name?"

Reluctantly, and making an effort to even say it aloud, she said, "Butch—but I hate that name, so I changed it to Joey."

"Well, I'm sorry. He doesn't like it and refuses to cooperate in obedience classes. How long have you had him?"

"Less than two months. I adopted him through someone I met at another show. His owners couldn't keep him any longer and I agreed to take him in. The first thing I did was to give him a new name. The second was to sign up for obedience classes. Although he was housebroken, obedient, and good-natured, he didn't pay attention during his obedience practice. When I read in the club's newsletter that you were going to be here, I thought you might be able to ask him questions and find out what's on his mind."

When I asked Butch what was on his mind, he told me, "I want to thank my new mom so much for making me feel comfortable. Tell her that it shows she's had experience with big dogs before. I can tell because she does special things for me, especially the way she raises my food bowls so that I don't have to reach all the way down to the floor. The way she treats me and the respect she gives me tell me that I've found a home where I can be happy and feel loved. That's all I ever wanted."

Naomi laughed and said, "I can't believe he's thanking me. But he's right. I do have a lot of experience with large dogs, especially Rottweilers. And yes, I have raised the food and water bowls to make things easier for him. So, understanding his point of view," she added with a laugh, "I guess it's back to being Butch."

As she gave him a big hug, I could see the beginning of a long loving and understanding relationship.

You may wonder how pets actually relate to their names. What is far more important than the sound you make when you use their name is the energy you project at them when you make that sound, for animals are much more sensitive to energy than are most humans, so they come to associate a feeling with that sound. When I was introduced to the cat Little Shit and heard that name, an involuntary feeling of mild revulsion ran through me, which the cat picked up and associated with his name.

My friend Tony has two dogs. The elder is an exalted old-soul black Labrador named Shiva; the other is a playful young-soul Labrador/pit bull mix named Louie. When Tony speaks Shiva's name, he projects the energy of respect and reverence toward the dog. When he speaks Louie's name, he projects energy that is light and goofy. Both energies suit, and both dogs are therefore happy with the sound Tony makes to get their attention.

Still on the subject of Shiva, he demonstrated to Tony just how much more our pets know than we give them credit for. Tony was worried about Shiva's hair loss on areas of his body and the way Shiva would scratch at the bald spots, so he asked both Shiva's vet and me about it. After examining Shiva, the vet said, "It's probably a food allergy. Let's try him on a special prescription low-protein diet for two weeks and see if there's any improvement."

Not knowing about Shiva's visit to the vet, about the same time, I had a talk with him and asked him about the hair loss. He told me, "It's an allergy to something I am eating. I think it's too much protein, so Tony should start by changing my diet."

Tony has always believed in my line of work, but that validation made him an absolute believer. And Shiva? He loved his new diet, stopped scratching immediately, and hair began growing back after only a few days.

What's In a Name?

Xena

Delia called me to talk to her 1½-year-old pug named Xena. Xena had been a rescue for Delia, who had met her when she was just four months old, abandoned and scared at the local shelter. Xena adjusted well in the beginning, sharing her home and her human with two other dogs: an eight-year-old pug and a very old Chihuahua mix who had been the queen at Delia's home for her entire life and whose peaceful and subdued personality made her an ideal lap dog.

It was only a couple of months into their relationship when Delia realized that Xena was taking over the turf. Delia felt good initially because she wanted Xena to feel more self-assured. She thought Xena was adjusting to her new life and reasoned that Xena must feel good in her home and love her very much since she was starting to feel jealous of the other dogs. By the time she called me, Xena was bossy and obnoxious to the older pets, oftentimes starting fights, pushing her way into their sleeping cushions, and growling and even biting at them when Delia had them on her lap.

It didn't take me long to find out that part of the problem originated in her name. Delia wanted Xena to become a warrior princess because she felt she needed to overcome her rough beginnings. Delia also allowed Xena to be overconfident by never giving her boundaries and by allowing Xena to run the household, instituting demands on Delia and the other dogs. For instance, she would not allow anyone on her mom's lap or on the bed. Walking her with the others was impossible and at meal times she needed to be segregated. It was getting to be too much for Delia.

Xena thought of herself as the warrior princess, full of attitude and in control. She would not allow Delia to be her boss, only her servant. We needed to change things.

Delia, at my suggestion, began to institute some control of her home, her sofas, and especially her bed. She decided to allow the fifteen-year-old Chihuahua to sleep on the bed because she was elderly and

27

didn't want Xena to stress her. Xena, on the other hand, needed to sleep on the floor of the bedroom, in her own cozy little bed, instead of feeling Mom was her property.

Next, I asked Delia to think of her not as a warrior princess but as a happy and well-adjusted member of the family who could share her time equally with the other pets and humans. I also had a heart-to-heart talk with Xena about needing a time-out when and if she displayed anger or possessiveness toward others. Delia also needed to assert herself as the alpha human while at the same time setting some boundaries on dog beds, food bowls, and particularly lap time.

Xena did blossom into a much better-liked member of the clan. Once her stubborn streak was addressed and redirected, she became a much-loved member of the family, regarded by everyone as a nurturing female without the warrior side.

As you can see, a name carries a lot of implications, but it is how we think about our animals when we call them that affects how they view themselves.

CHAPTER 3

Do Animals Have Souls?

$\int$ ome religions understand that all humans are beings of light and that our primary identity is one of an eternal soul, which continues after death and chooses to come back with different personalities so as to evolve, learn, and grow until perfect. When each cycle of lifetimes is completed, the soul returns to the divine source from which it originated for renewal and revitalization.

Throughout history, the world's religions have debated whether animals possess souls. One school of thought, mostly from Eastern religions such as Jainism, says that animal souls are equal in all respects to human souls. At the other extreme are faiths such as Christianity that reserve the immortal soul for righteous humans.

Judaism believes there are different levels of soul. The lowest level, *nefesh*, is the animal soul, the breathing, functioning part that leaves at death. The highest level of soul, reserved for humans, is *neshuma*, the spiritual part that lives forever connected with God.

Buddhists refer to the "thread of karma," the chain of life, a continuity of constant becoming. They believe every life form has intelligence and worth, whether it is a rock, a dog, an ant, or a human. They say that animals are living the same lives that humans live, and that they have spirits, as do humans.

Many faiths believe man is spiritually superior to animals, and this has profoundly affected the way man has treated the animal world and environment. Separating animals from the highest realm has made it easier to use them for food, fashion, medical experiments, and sport. This notion that animals don't have souls was bolstered by the Bible's Genesis 1:26 that tells us, "Let them have dominion over the fish of the sea, over the birds of the air and over the cattle, over all the earth and over every creeping thing on the earth." However, the word "dominion" comes from the root Hebrew word *yorade*, which means "to have communion with."

Think for a second what would have happened to animals over the centuries if the Bible had told us to have communion *with* them, rather than dominion *over* them!

So many times in my consultations, pet owners who are grieving the loss of a beloved animal ask, "Do you think I'll see him again? Does she have a soul? Will he go to heaven? Will she come back to me again?"

Do Animals Have Souls?

All I know is what the animals tell me. Generally, the essence of the animal's personality while on earth remains around us so that we are able to contact them after their death. Many times they meet up with or even live with the souls of their human loved ones on the other side. They are always around and glad to be able to communicate their feelings with us.

After talking to many of them, I have no doubt that there is a place, or vibration, or state of being where they go and remain after physical death. They can describe the place, they know the reasons for them being there, and they know their purpose, both for being here on earth and once they've crossed over.

As we see in the following stories, every animal is an individual and has his or her own outlook.

Sailor

A few years ago, I went to see Todd, who had called me three days after Sailor, his cat of twenty-one years, had passed away. He was in terrible grief and told me, "If only I could talk to Sailor's spirit and ask his forgiveness, I'll feel a little better."

The day was typical for Southern California, beautiful and sunny; because Todd lived on the coast in a bright and airy little house, the temperature was agreeable too. I sat on the same sofa that Sailor, a beautiful Himalayan seal point male with blue eyes, had spent much of his life lying on. Star, another Himalayan, a seventeen-year-old female, shy and unimpressed by my visit, lay snoozing under the coffee table.

Todd showed me dozens of letters and cards of condolence he had received from friends and coworkers. He had them all displayed on the kitchen table with a picture of Sailor in the middle. He was grieving openly and took no pains to hide his obvious distress. Knowing a little of what I do, Todd told me, "I just want to explain things to Sailor and tell him how much I miss him."

I readily saw and heard Sailor, for he was still very much around the house and his presence was very strong. He was unable to move on because Todd's grief was holding him back, but he had glimpsed the soul plane and told me, "It's a beautiful place, full of light and vivid colors that I've never seen before and can't even begin to describe."

Todd asked Sailor if he had seen Rick, Todd's friend who had passed on.

"Yes, for a little while," Sailor answered. "He is in a higher vibration than me and is very busy."

Without being prompted by Todd, Sailor talked about his final hours. "I was sick for a while and refused food and water. I was so tired that I just wanted to let go of my body but Todd wouldn't hear of it. He tried to force me to drink, but couldn't do much about the food. I was very, very tired but now I feel free and am fine. Tell Todd that I chose to go at that moment. I had to wait for him to leave the room or else I couldn't have done it."

When I conveyed this to the distraught Todd, he explained, "I'd been home all day with Sailor at my side. I knew something was terribly wrong with him. He wasn't eating or drinking and his eyes were fixed on the horizon. Then, in the late afternoon, I got a phone call from a customer, went into another room where the paperwork was, and spent about ten minutes on the phone. When I returned to the living room, I saw that Sailor wasn't where I left him. He'd jumped down from the sofa, gone into the back yard, and was lying on the cool dirt under the lemon tree. He was gone."

After a moment to compose himself, Todd continued, "If only I hadn't taken that phone call . . . if I'd just stayed in the living room . . ."

"But that is exactly what Sailor wanted," I told him. "He wanted to die alone and he needed to do it fast. He didn't want to see your face and feel your heart aching. He made his final effort to die by himself in silence, away from his dear friend and the house he knew."

I could feel that Todd understood Sailor's reasoning. He asked, "Is Sailor coming back to me? And if so, where should I look and when?"

Sailor immediately said, "Yes, I will come back, but Todd will have to wait a while. I would like to pick exactly the same breed because I like the beauty. Tell him that when the time is right, he will know it in his heart."

As Todd assimilated this, Sailor went on. "When Todd is asleep, I lie on the pillow and try to communicate with him in his dreams. And I like to stand by the doorway and look out into the back yard, as I used to do. But most of all, I love to hover around the kitchen when he's feeding Star."

I conveyed all this to Todd and added, "It seems that Sailor can't disconnect from the fact that he no longer needs food for nourishment but still longs for a good meal, so he watches you preparing Star's food instead."

Sailor then said, "Tell Todd that he is surrounded by guardian angels. So many, in fact, that I sometimes have a hard time getting close to him." Sailor accompanied this message with a humorous movie clip of him pushing his way through the angelic host, saying, "Excuse me, pardon me, excuuuuussse me," as he tries to open a way through to his friend.

Sailor also asked, "Tell Todd that Star will always be aloof and in need of her own space. She won't change her attitude just because I'm no longer there. She asks for love and attention on her terms, and that's her way."

Todd nodded. "Yes, he's right. Star is aloof and quite different from Sailor. And I think you're right about him trying to come to me in my dreams. When I'm lying down in bed, I feel Sailor's presence next to me on the pillow."

Todd was pleased with the session, so I bade him and Star farewell.

Six months later, an elated Todd called to tell me, "I had a dream about Sailor and, when I woke up, I just knew it was time to go looking for him. So I called everyone I could think of, like the animal shelters, rescue groups, and humane societies in the area. Finally, I reached the animal shelter near my home. You'll laugh at this. I asked if they had a long-haired Himalayan male, seal point, blue eyes, neutered, declawed front paws, between one and two years old."

I did indeed laugh because such a specific description sounded ridiculous. "But guess what," Todd said. "The woman on the other end said, 'Yes, I have one just like you describe. Would you like to come see him?' Well, it didn't take me but fifteen minutes to get there. And when I saw him, it was love at first sight, so I brought him home."

"That's amazing, Todd," I said.

"It gets better," he said. "The first night, I noticed that the new cat had all Sailor's habits, including climbing on the sofa and sleeping on the arm next to me while I watch TV. The next morning, it was just the same, with him doing exactly what Sailor used to do. And Star just goes about her business as if the new cat in the house is the same one she'd grown up with. After a week of watching him, I'm convinced that it really is Sailor and that everything is back the way it should be. I just wanted to let you know that I believe Sailor's desire to come back to me was so strong that he made it happen, just as you said he would."

"That's wonderful. Congratulations."

"Oh, and I've named him Sailor, too."

How can it be, you might wonder, that the new Sailor was over a year old, but only six months had elapsed after the first Sailor died? One of two things happened here. The first has to do with time being meaningless on the soul plane. A soul can incarnate anywhere along the timeline, even in what is history to us on the physical plane. So it's quite possible for Sailor's soul to have reincarnated six months earlier than his crossing over.

The second possibility is the "walk-in" phenomenon. By agreement with a soul already in a body, it leaves and a new soul walks in. The first soul may just have wanted to experience life as a kitten and is ready to leave, either through death or a "walk-out." The incoming soul may want to avoid the messy kitten or puppy stage and just get on with life as a young adult. (This happens a lot in humans, when an evolved soul doesn't need to experience the lengthy growing-up years and just wants to get on with its spiritual mission. By taking on a body that is grown, it can get on with life more quickly.) Many walk-ins happen as the animal or person lies on the verge of death, whether by accident or incurable disease. The person or animal then recuperates miraculously—further evidence of a walk-in.

In addition to their own agenda, animals also walk in to support or teach us certain lessons, speed up our learning, or make us more human.

Lady

In the previous chapter, we met Lady, one of my Shih Tzu females. She is an example of a walk-in/walk-out.

I'd been with her from the beginning, watching her birth. I'd even cut her umbilical cord because her mother, Princess, was unable to bite through it. For two years, we'd been inseparable, and I knew her intimately. She was shy and calm, had very short hair for a Shih Tzu (unlike her parents), spent countless hours on my lap, ate very slowly, never, ever barked, and never licked people, especially on the face.

As we saw, she wanted to find another family to live with so that she could be "special." A week after Mr. and Mrs. Woodbridge took her, they returned to finalize the paperwork and I got a chance to ask Lady some questions.

35

Lady shared with me her story. "I made a pact with their first dog, Youshie. I wanted to find a new family and Youshie wanted to release her tired body. Youshie knew it was her time to go but had trouble making the decision. You thought I could have some beautiful babies but, after my first litter, you were convinced that I didn't enjoy motherhood so you had me spayed. Youshie and I waited until the right moment so that her soul could come into this body."

I had to think back. Lady was spayed on June 3 and Youshie died on June 17, just two weeks later. Since the physical body needed to be in good health for the transition to take effect right away, it made sense to me that they waited two weeks. Three months later, the couple came to my house and met Lady, which had given Youshie's soul the time needed to walk into Lady's body. That immediately explained why the dog had behaved so out-of-character. I'd been shocked when Lady had licked Mr. Woodbridge's face, but now realized that it hadn't been Lady at all. Youshie's soul was already occupying Lady's body. Now it all made perfect sense.

Two weeks later, Lois Woodbridge wrote to me:

Dear Monica,

We have had Youshie for only thirteen days and she has fit right in. To say we adore her is putting it mildly. She is such a loving little thing and seems to just want to be with us all of the time. She and Woody [his nickname] are totally bonded. If he moves, she moves. Because she follows him everywhere he goes, her nickname is "Glue."

You know, we were looking for a puppy, and never gave a thought to an older dog. We had looked from San Bernardino to Riverside and all over around here. Yours was the last place we knew of to look before we would have had to start waiting for people to call us about new litters.

Woody and I talk about the fact that when we first saw Lady, we both had the same thought at the same time because she looked so much like the dog we had. And who could deny the fact that she picked out Woody when she jumped up on the couch, went to him, got into his lap, stared into his eyes, and licked his face? Even when we took her home that first day, she got into the car, wasn't agitated in the slightest, settled down in my lap and rode quietly to our house. It was like she was telling us that she was happy to have a new home with us. Odd, too, that you had Lady spayed just two weeks before we lost our Youshie.

Anyway, there can be no doubt in my mind that we were meant to have that dog and that everything worked out so that we would find her and that she has, in every way, told us that she is completely content.

Then a month later, I received another letter:

Dear Monica,

I just wanted to let you know that Youshie is totally our dog. She has taken over the house, our bed and the yard. She loves our big yard, it is like her own jungle. She races around under the bushes and she and my husband play catch or she runs after the plastic golf balls that he hits to her with his golf club. And she barks at the neighbor's cat.

When Woody comes home, she just goes crazy, jumping on him, running around, getting a toy to bring him, and he hugs and pets her. I get the same kind of greeting when I come home.

She is such a loving dog. In the evening, she is always either in one of our laps or lying on our feet, and right in the middle of the bed when it's time to go to sleep. We just adore her and she is glued to my husband. When I ask her, "Where's Dad?"

Do Animals Have Souls?

she perks up, looks at me and goes dashing off to find him. She helps him all day when he is working in the yard.

Anyway, there is no doubt in our minds that she is supposed to be our dog and we know that she is totally happy with us, so you found her just the right home.

Face-licking, barking, and chasing around are all things Lady *never* did, but which the Woodbridges told me the first Youshie used to do. That convinced me that the soul of Youshie did indeed walk into Lady's body sometime during the three months between Youshie's death and the Woodbridges first coming to see me. She also grew a new coat of beautiful long hair, as you can see in her picture (page 23), just like her predecessor.

The speed with which Youshie acclimated to her new body amazed me. When a new soul arrives in the body, it can spend up to a year becoming fully functional and at ease, depending on how much affinity both souls have (i.e., how similar they are in such things as magnetic resonance and aura). Youshie seemed to take very little time to adjust to Lady's body, although I visited her three months later and she still recognized my scent.

The next story is also about a dog who had made the transition to the other side, and I was surprised by the specific descriptions of her life while here on earth.

Molly

There is always something new for me to learn from animals and this session was very special because of the details I received. Toni had made an appointment so that I could talk to Molly, her two-year-old female pit bull. When I arrived, I was greeted enthusiastically by a German shepherd and a pit bull puppy about four months old. Puzzled, I asked Toni, "Wasn't I was supposed to talk to a two-year-old pit bull named Molly?"

Toni gave me a picture of Molly. "So I take it that Molly isn't here," I asked, getting the familiar feeling of emptiness when I sense that the animal is no longer on this plane.

"Molly died unexpectedly and I need to get some closure," Toni said.

As soon as I started the consultation with Molly, she sent me an image of herself locked up in an apartment for a long period of time. There was no food or water, and she showed me her having to eat the wooden cabinets as the only source of nourishment. She conveyed that she'd been very hungry. The grim pictures continued, showing urine and feces all over the floors, kitchen, living room, everywhere. Molly had been too scared and too weak to bark any more. Her time was up.

Toni was surprised at the specific and graphic images and explained, "I got Molly through the pit bull rescue foundation. The police found her in an empty apartment, and she was just skin and bones. She'd been starved and left for dead. Her story was in all the newspapers and on the television news. I had to wait six weeks before she was well enough to come home with me. They kept her in foster care until her weight returned to normal. I visited her frequently and we became really close. She was a pit bull with a heart of gold, as if she knew she'd been given a second chance."

Molly continued to describe her experiences. "I was not supposed to live beyond that time. But after I met Toni at the Rescue Foster Parent Home, I decided to stick around because of the love and affection I sensed she could bring into my life. I wanted to experience the love I never knew before and was willing to stick it out for a while. I was able to put on weight but I had a lesion on my heart caused by malnutrition and it never healed. Tell Toni that I went smoothly, without pain, and best of all, it was very fast. Tell her, too, that I am so thankful to her for having given me almost two years of peace, love, and unconditional attention, catering to my every need and desire. I never before had that kind of love and am so glad I decided to stay around a little bit longer. But my time was up, and I needed to go when I did."

Toni was crying but, through her tears, she managed to explain. "A couple of weeks ago, I left the house to go to the bank. I was only gone ten minutes and, when I got back, I saw that Molly had a bite on her neck that was bleeding profusely. Another pit bull that I was fostering had done it. I rushed her to the nearest vet, only seven minutes away. He said that the bite wasn't life-threatening but did need stitches under anesthetic. Molly died from the anesthesia on the operating table that afternoon without regaining consciousness."

Molly said, "My heart was weak and couldn't survive the anesthetic."

Molly

Toni told me several times, "My heart is aching because I feel I missed something, that I could have done more. Also the former foster mom is blaming me for Molly's death. The feeling of guilt is drowning me in tears and sorrow."

Poor Toni was feeling dreadfully guilty about what happened and was punishing herself for her lack of foresight. "Maybe I should have stayed with her. Maybe I should have never had another pit bull in the house. Maybe I should have gone to my regular vet and not the closest one. Maybe I should have told her more often how much I loved her. Maybe . . ."

After this consultation, Toni felt much better and was able to manage her grief and give closure to her guilty feelings. But Molly will always be in Toni's mind and heart.

Molly's story reveals that our animals know when it is their time to go. Sometimes they even warn us, as we see in the next story.

Fleas

I met Karen and her daughter Jennifer after Fleas, their male Golden Retriever mix, had died. They also needed some closure. Fleas had been with them for most of his seventeen years. He had been their family dog and had moved in with Jennifer when she took her first apartment.

When I contacted Fleas, he said, "I feel incredibly young and vibrant now that I've released my body. Everything was hurting and I made a decision that it was time to go. Jennifer couldn't accept this and kept trying to feed me different things. Somehow I needed to tell Karen, Jennifer, and her boyfriend, John, whom I also loved, that I was ready to leave.

"I figured that I had to do something out of the ordinary so one day when everyone was together talking and I was lying on my own bed, I stood up, went to each of them, and kissed them gently, allowing them to pet my head. I moved slowly, without hurrying, looking deeply into each of their eyes and saying my goodbyes. Then I turned around and went back to my bed. I closed my eyes and never opened them again."

Jennifer asked tearfully, "Is he coming back to me as another pet?"

When I asked him, Fleas said clearly and forcefully, "NO!" (He really did! I actually heard the word "no" in my mind.) Poor Jennifer was so upset that she asked me three other times and his answer was the same each time. On the third occasion, he added, "I've decided not to come back to her. I plan to stay on this side and work with her from here, much like a guardian angel."

(Sometimes, my own feelings get in the way. I wanted so much to give Jennifer some hope of reincarnation but Fleas denied me the opportunity each time. Breaking the sad news to her was difficult, especially since most of the time when we have a special relationship with our pets, they do come back to us in a different body.)

As if trying to explain himself, on the fourth occasion, Fleas sent me an image of him waiting for Jennifer at the end of her life. He was the first to greet her, but behind him was a long line of animals (mostly dogs) filling the tunnel of light.

I didn't understand the image because there were far too many animals for one person to have in one lifetime. Nevertheless, I tried to translate my picture as it came through. "You're still young and your path in this lifetime is probably not yet decided. Perhaps later in life, you'll be in a position to help a lot of animals, maybe in the veterinary field or rescuing animals. Fleas has chosen to remain on the other side to help you make important decisions regarding all those animals, and they will be there to thank you when you cross over. Fleas considers his mission so important that he isn't coming back in the flesh."

As an afterthought, I asked Jennifer, "What do you do now for work?"

"I'm a dog groomer."

It all fell into place then. I knew she was destined to help a lot of creatures with her understanding, love, and gentleness. And Fleas would be right beside her to help and guide her in every way.

Samantha

Once a month, I hold an open house at the Learning Light Foundation in Anaheim, California, during which I give fifteen-minute consultations. I invite everyone to come in with their pets or pictures of them for a quick "talk." Often they are very successful. One of my clients had been so impressed by a previous session with me that she'd returned with her mother and sister.

The sister's name was Sue and she had brought some photographs with her and wanted to know what I could tell her about her cats. One was a gray 8½-year-old female tabby named Samantha, or Sam for short. The other was a nine-year-old male orange tabby named Toby.

As soon as Sue showed me the picture of Sam, I asked her, "Is the cat still with you?" Startled by my question, she said, "Yes, so far!"

I relayed to her, "Sam is telling me that she's very sick, always on medication. But she wants to talk about another cat that you had, who looked exactly like her. Did you once have cat who looked like Samantha?"

Sue replied, "Yes, I did, but it was quite a few years back. I remember her very well. Her name was Macy."

"Well," I said to Sue, "Sam is telling me that she is the same soul as Macy. She came back to complete her work. She feels she went too soon and that you also took care of Macy when she was sick."

Sue nodded. "Yes, Macy had cancer and was euthanized."

"Sam is telling me that she knows that in this lifetime she has a job to do. She knows that she is back here as a teacher for you. Patience and the ability to care for someone on a long-term basis is something you need to learn, internalize, and practice without complaining. This is Sam's purpose in this lifetime and she knows it. There is nothing that makes Sam happier than spending quality time with you."

During this time, Sue listened silently. I think she was amazed to learn that the souls of Macy and Sam had a soul agreement with her to teach her something that would help her in the future. I couldn't tell her what this was, only that it has to do with learning patience and the ability to care for others, especially family.

Sam added, "Sue is doing a good job and I am happy with my choice to have come back in this lifetime as her cat. If there is one thing I would like to request, it's that Sue spend more time with me and is able to speak to me out loud."

Sue told me, "Even though my family and I have had many, many cats in the home, I've never known a cat quite like Samantha before. She's been a sick girl all her life but is never angry or upset and never fights with any of my other cats. She is the perfect lady. Also, she's the only cat I know of who takes her medicine readily. She opens her mouth and swallows the pills all by herself. And she needs to do this several times a day with different pills."

"Pilling a cat can be hazardous to your health," I joked.

Sue added, "I'm really impressed by this session. I feel a little bit guilty for not giving Samantha the attention she was hoping for and I promise to change my ways. Thank you so much."

I smiled. Little Sam had made an impression on her that she would not readily forget.

CHAPTER 4

Messages from the Other Side

Some people are able to connect with the souls of those who have crossed over to the other side. Medium John Edward does precisely this on his show *Crossing Over with John Edward*. And many times, the souls who contact audience members through John report that a beloved family pet is also with them on the other side. Other well-known mediums include James Van Praagh, author of *Talking to Heaven*; Dannion Brinkley, author of *Saved by the Light*; and my personal favorite, Sylvia Browne, often seen on the *Montel Williams Show* and the author of several books.

The Yorkie

One day, after a talk I gave on pet communication at the Learning Light Foundation, many people told me how they enjoyed it and that they agreed with what I had to say. One woman joked, "My dog is perfect except that he'll be in the spare bedroom, bark once, run out of that room into the hall, come up to me and just stare at me. I would be a happy woman if I just knew why."

I joined in the good-natured laughter about the odd quirks our pets have but suddenly stopped, hardly able to believe what I was seeing. Completely unbidden, a movie had just started running on my inner screen. I was looking through the eyes of a dog, which I somehow knew to be a Yorkie.

Oddly, I am seeing both my surroundings and "me" as a dog in a hallway. To my right is a room with a shaft of sunlight angling in through the window with a dresser in front of it. On the dresser are doilies and a neatly arranged comb-and-mirror set. To my left, I see a perfectly made bed with a beautiful cover that looks to be handmade. Everything is meticulous and clean, as if nothing has been touched in a long time. I get the sense that an old lady slept there. Apart from that, the room is empty.

I am suddenly drawn into the room and see to my right in a corner a figure that appears to be made of light, ghostly and shimmering. The figure is somehow floating higher than a normal person would. I feel impelled to approach so that I can inspect this thing. As I get closer and raise my head, I can tell that it's an old lady dressed in white. Her brilliant energy is full of love for me. I hear her thought: "Come closer," and I do. I sense that the dog's love for her is very strong as she sends him/me love through her caressing eyes and warm energy. She even touches him/me lightly. I sense the dog's thrill at her touch. Then she fades and is gone, but I am so full of radiant joy that I bark my hello/goodbye and rush out to the hallway to tell my second mom that I've seen my first mom, that she's here. But my second mom just looks at me and does not understand me. *Oh, well, maybe next time,* I think. So I walk back into the hall and go look for something else to do.

The movie lasted just a few seconds; suddenly I was back in the room, once more aware of all the chatter around me. Turning to the woman, I said, "Would you mind if I asked you a question?"

She nodded, so I asked, "Have you recently lost a close member of your family?"

Her hand flew to her mouth in surprise. She replied, "Why, yes. My mother died recently. How did you know?"

As I related my vision from her Yorkie, her eyes filled with tears. When I'd finished, she started sobbing uncontrollably. I felt bad because we'd all just been joking around and now she couldn't hold back her grief.

She tried to talk but couldn't, so she motioned for me to wait until she'd composed herself. Then half talking, half crying, she told me, "My mother had been sick for a long time and was living with me in the spare bedroom. You described the room perfectly. The dresser, the handmade quilt and everything. I haven't been able to go into that room at all in the three months she's been gone, which is why it looks untouched.

"The Yorkie was my mother's dog, and I'm now taking care of him. I know he's been very sad after my mom's passing and misses her a lot. I had no idea that he can see her spirit but it makes perfect sense to me now because his odd behavior started only after her passing. Also, recently I've been wondering whether there's an afterlife. It's somehow fitting that my mother's little dog is the one to bring me the answer."

I was fascinated at how the universe intervened in this way because that type of remote sensing is not something I usually do. I generally need to see the pet in person, or at least a photo, before I can establish contact. I also need to know the pet's name and get to know the people involved. In this case, however, I knew nothing about any of them.

This story also raises an interesting point. When someone in the family dies outside the home—in the hospital, say—the household pets will be confused by the sudden absence, as we've just seen. So what can you do?

First the animal needs to be told, whether by talking out loud or by sending them an image. Mourning in front of your pets also helps because they instinctively pick up your sorrow and the image lets them understand why. When sending an image of the person not coming back, you can visualize the person as if he or she was leaving for the day. If they're merely away on a trip, show the person in another environment, followed by their return.

If the person is dead, show images to your pet of the person being buried and the soul elevating into the spirit world. Do this on a quiet day with your animal by your side. It is important to "visualize" a movie as it plays out in your head, because our animals read our thoughts and our pictures. Many people tell me that it is impossible for them to visualize a moving picture. Most can visualize colors, so explain the situation out loud and visualize purple, the color of the seventh chakra and, it is said, the direct path to our higher self.

As the next story reveals, animals are incredible creatures with great sensibility and vision. They never cease to amaze me.

Ebony

Mary called me desperately seeking advice about Ebony, her female eight-year-old miniature poodle. "She's losing weight for no reason.

And being only five or six pounds to begin with, I'm really worried. Can you tell me what's going on?"

When I am called in for any reason that could involve a physical condition, I insist on the animal having a complete physical from a vet. Only then can I feel confident that we are talking about a behavioral or psychological problem. So I told Mary to have her vet check Ebony out. Two days later, Mary called back. "The vet ran a complete blood panel on Ebony and there's nothing physically wrong with her. He told me he thinks that Ebony is depressed."

When I walked in the house, Ebony was so happy to have company that she immediately started running around the living room, doing figure eights and playing hide-and-seek with me. She also brought in some of her kibble, which she munched eagerly while Mary and I discussed her case.

Mary showed me Ebony's play toys and bed, and gave me a quick tour of the house, which, although absolutely beautiful and with a breathtaking view of the Pacific Ocean, was lonely and cold. A little like its owner, I thought. Mary had lost her husband of thirty-three years about a year before after nursing him through a 2½-year illness of pancreatic and liver cancer.

Initially, Mary had shared all her time with Ebony, but lately had been seeing more of her girlfriends during the day. However, she made a point of never leaving Ebony alone for more than six hours at a time.

When I first started talking to Ebony, she said, "All I want is for Mom to be happy again. I feel sad because Mom is lonely. I want to play more and be with Mom more. I'd like to go to the park, or someplace fun. I also love my food, my toys, and my Mom, but I miss my Dad. I was Daddy's little girl."

Mary confirmed this. "Ebony used to spend all her time on Dad's bed while he was sick, often cradled in his arms for comfort. After he died, she never again went into the bedroom."

49

When Ebony started talking about her dad, she sent me some very vivid images as if in an introduction. She said, "Look, this is my daddy."

I saw a tall, distinguished, imposing man standing next to Ebony. His full head of gray hair was combed all the way back, and he wore a suit. He looked to be very intelligent and dignified, his commanding presence demanding respect. His eyes, however, were soft and full of tenderness and humor, although there was in them a glint of power and knowing. I carefully described him to Mary, who interrupted, "Yes, that's him! That's my husband."

Encouraged by this, I continued to watch the inner movie. Mary's husband told me, "I have wanted to communicate with Mary for a long time, as I promised I would. This is the perfect opportunity for me to come through, thanks to Ebony, who is always aware of my visits. Please tell Mary that I am working hard to find her some other man who she will like, and that I am very close to doing just that."

Continuing to speak through me, he joked, "You're very picky, Mary, and arranging the right timing with the right person has been difficult. So please be patient for a little while longer."

Mary chuckled, as she knew perfectly well that he was right. She had a lot of questions, of course. "How old is this man? How handsome? How wealthy? When will this happen and how will I know it's him?"

He answered most of her questions, but joked, "I won't tell you all the specifics. I want *you* to do some work, too."

Mary then asked me, "Could you ask Ebony if she really can see her daddy?"

Ebony replied, "Yes, I talk with him often. Sometimes in the middle of the night I see him next to the bed. Then I go to the kitchen and get a kibble, and come back to the bedroom just to watch Mom and Dad."

I laughed at the image; it reminded me of the human habit of munching popcorn while watching a movie. I loved little Ebony's great sense of humor.

Ebony

Ebony thanks me after our session.

This consultation worked well for both of them. Mary got over her sadness and had a new outlook on life, happy that her husband had made good on his promise to communicate with her from the other side. And Ebony, over her depression about her mom being sad, resumed eating normally.

Although I no longer do private consultations for humans, I was glad I was able to translate for them. The images came in so strongly, and it was so important for Mary to hear what her husband had to say, that I couldn't deny them the pleasure of knowing that he was around and working toward her happiness. And little Ebony was the bridge that made this possible.

Few of us realize the depth of an animal's grief at the loss of its human companion. If we are not observant and miss the subtle clues that they give us, then we can only rely on someone else to bring this to light. I am honored that my gift allows me to do this, as in the next story.

Cindy

I teach animal communication classes at the Learning Light Foundation in Anaheim and, once a month, I do consultations all day. On one such occasion, I was visited by Cindy, a nine-year-old German shepherd, who came in with her human companions, two sisters, Janice and Sharon. Janice, whom I'd met before, told me, "Cindy is Sharon's dog. I arranged for this consultation as a gift to her."

Cindy was hyper at first, crying and whining all the time, and looking everywhere. She obviously wanted to leave and refused to make eye contact with me. Sharon said, "This goes on all the time. What is wrong with her?"

Cindy, although uncomfortable, started to complain almost right away. "My mom abandoned me. I look for her everywhere but can't find her."

When I translated this to Sharon, she said, "That can't be. Admittedly, I go to work, but Cindy shouldn't feel abandoned because of that."

I turned back to Cindy, who said, "It has nothing to do with her going to work. I just have this emptiness inside me. I feel lonely."

Because I'd felt this emptiness before in other animals, I asked Sharon, "Has anyone, human or animal, left the house recently?"

Sharon replied, "Yes, my mother passed away last year. Cindy was her dog. I moved back into the house with my daughter. Because Cindy stayed in the same house, I didn't think my mother's death would have much of an effect on the dog."

Knowing better, I turned back to Cindy, who repeated, "I'm really upset at being abandoned by my mom."

"Cindy," I asked, "do you realize that your mom is dead?"

Cindy replied, "No, I don't."

Sharon confirmed this. "Our mother took ill suddenly and was rushed to the hospital, where she died. To Cindy, I guess she just disappeared one day."

Cindy still had doubts, however. "I can still smell Mom everywhere in the house, especially in the bedroom closet. She must be coming back, otherwise why are her clothes still there?"

Sharon admitted, "Cindy's right. We still haven't packed up Mom's clothes or cleaned out the closet. That's why her scent is still so strong in the house."

Cindy also complained, "My mom used to talk to me all the time but now no one talks to me."

Sharon chuckled when I relayed this information. "It's true. Mom talked to Cindy all the time, as if she were a third daughter. I hardly talk at all. That's just my personality, but I'll make a real effort to change since it's important to Cindy."

Using images, I explained to Cindy, "Your Mom has gone to another plane of existence but she still watches over you. You need not look for her anymore. You were not abandoned and Sharon loves you a great deal. And she promises to talk a lot more to you from now on."

On hearing this, Cindy settled down in front of us, becoming quiet and calm. She laid her face down between her front paws and looked at me. When I finished the session, she slowly sat up, came over to me, and put her face on my lap as her way of saying thanks.

Sometimes one animal will act as a messenger for an animal friend, as in the next story.

Jarreau

Robin called me to talk about Jarreau, her black, female, fourteen-year-old cat who had to take asthma medication daily.

Jarreau was initially withdrawn and wanted nothing to do with me but, after a while, she thawed and decided that talking to me would be okay. Once she opened up, she told me, "I'm concerned about Mom.

She needs to go out more often and enjoy life more. I want her so much to be happy."

Jarreau continued, "I was sad at first when I lost my friend, and Mom was worried about me. I want Mom to know that I'm fine and much prefer to be alone and number one."

As I relayed this to Robin, I had no idea what the cat was talking about, and she didn't volunteer any information except to say, "Yes, I lost an animal about six months ago."

Turning back to Jarreau, we talked about her food, going out to the patio, and the hot days. She sent me a picture of an ice cube in her water, with her pawing and playing with it. "Jarreau is asking me to ask you to put ice cubes in her water on hot days. Did you used to do this?" I asked Robin.

"Yes, when Jarreau was a kitten, I used to put an ice cube in her water all the time."

I replied, "Based on the pictures she's showing me, she misses that."

Just as we were finishing, I told Robin, "Someone is here visiting. It's a beautiful cat sitting in a very regal pose. She has orange and black lines down her body—a kind of tiger look. Also, her face looks like a little round heart. Do you recognize her?"

An excited Robin exclaimed, "Yes! It's my other female, Mariah! The one who passed away six months ago."

Mariah told me, "I just wanted to come back and say hello. Tell Robin that I love her very much and want her to know that I'm still around, loving and taking care of her. I visit her often. Since you can see me, will you tell Robin that I'm okay?"

Robin confirmed, "Many times I feel Mariah around, rubbing against my legs, and her presence next to me. I know it's her, because Jarreau will be in the other room."

I was delighted for Robin that Mariah came in so unexpectedly. It gave the reading a whole new meaning for her because she didn't know that contact could be made with a pet that's crossed over. It gave me validation that the ones we love are still looking out for us and continue to love us even if we don't see them.

As an animal communicator, I need validation just as much as my clients do. Sometimes my skepticism makes me my own worst enemy. Translating the love that transcends planes might be easy but personalizing the animals to my human clients is not. It is important for animals to know that their humans get their messages, and it's important for me to know that it is their particular departed pet who is really doing the talking. That's when translating the right pictures comes into play, as happened with my description of Mariah, and in the next story, where the pet made quite sure his mom knew it was him.

Rocky

Alice e-mailed me regarding the loss of Rocky, her 1½-year-old Pomeranian (see photo, page 56). She told me that not only was she grieving the loss of her beloved Rocky but that she also blamed herself for his death. Rocky had ingested a rubber band that became lodged in his stomach and, even though he'd been operated on, he died two days later. Alice was devastated and needed to find solace, maybe even forgiveness.

The very first image that I received when I connected with Rocky through his photo was of a tiny Pomeranian standing on his rear legs, jumping up and down, at the same time spinning around and moving his front paws. While I savored this cute image in my mind, I heard the command, "Before you start, it's important for you to tell her what I am doing!"

Startled by Rocky's insistence, I told Alice, "Rocky wants me to describe to you what I'm seeing because it's important."

As I did, Alice laughed and said, "That's him, that really is him. He always used to greet me by dancing as soon as I opened the door."

This confirmed for Alice that we really were communicating with Rocky, and he came through with many more details of their short time together. The most important message was, "I'm feeling just fine and happy to be able to dance again. I know I was mischievous and doing something I wasn't supposed to when I ate that 'string.' Most important, though, I don't blame you for my death. My job was to teach you how to be independent and at the same time care for someone else. You made your family proud by showing them you were able to do this."

Alice confirmed that she had just moved out of her parents' house and was living alone for the first time. Her parents, though supportive of her, did not think she was ready to take care of herself, let alone someone else's needs. Thanks to Rocky, she'd been able to prove them wrong.

Rocky

The Pomeranian who made sure his mom knew he was still dancing on the other side.

This and the previous chapters show that not only do our pets survive physical death but they also remain in close contact with us. Psychic medium John Edward often ends his *Crossing Over* show by telling us to appreciate and validate those important relationships in our lives so that someone like him doesn't have to do it for us.

I agree. Waste no opportunity. Let every encounter with your pets be a loving one, for you never know when it might be the last. Mirror back to them some of the enormous love they have in their hearts for you, even from across the veil.

CHAPTER 5

Death and Euthanasia, or "It's Okay to Cry"

I cry much of the time during consultations. I can't help it. When my heart is open and my mind is in receiving mode, I am unable to control my feelings during the free flow between animal and human. My body often becomes a sponge for an animal's feelings and it's not unusual for my clients to see me with my eyes closed, tears flowing freely down my cheeks.

Animals don't cry as we do, but their feelings of love are so strong that I cry from the sheer emotional intensity. That may be difficult to understand for someone who is not an emotional empath, but please trust me—feeling love that intensely is almost a religious experience.

The hardest aspect of my work is talking to clients about the death of their beloved pets, either naturally or by euthanasia, yet I am compelled to do it. Why? Because I believe I provide a service that few others can. I made a promise to myself and the universe that if I am to have this gift, I will use it to the best of my ability and will not let it go to waste just because some aspects of the job are painful. As long as I can bring people some comfort, get their questions answered, and give closure to their suffering, I know I am doing my job.

Without question, the death of an animal friend is a huge loss. People who have never known the joy of a close bond with an animal companion may not understand the depth of that loss. They may downplay the importance with, "It was only a dog. Just get another one," as if a new pet could somehow make you forget the old one or take away the pain. You have every right to grieve the loss of your friend. In fact, psychologists know that the loss of a beloved pet triggers the same stages of grief as the loss of a human loved one.

Along with the grief of loss, people might also get stuck in anger ("Damn him for running into traffic!") or guilt ("Why didn't I see the lump before?" or "If only I'd taken him to the vet sooner!").

In each consultation, animals continue to teach me more about death and dying. We all could learn a great deal from them if we would only listen to what they have to say. In the first story, a dog is a perfect mirror for her mom.

Lulu

Tanya called me about Lulu, her Old English sheepdog, a five-year-old female who was dying of cancer (see photograph, page 62). Two of her

---

Death and Euthanasia, or "It's Okay to Cry"

teats had already been removed, and the cancer had advanced into her lungs. Tanya struck me as a grounded, centered woman, learned in the ways of the universe. She was serious and reserved, as if she had an attitude of detachment, more like a "show me before I tell." Medically, Tanya knew everything the veterinarians had told her but, mentally and emotionally, she was hoping to learn more about her friend.

When I arrived, Lulu, a gentle giant, was lying on her pillow in the living room. She stood to greet me, and then all three of us sat down on the floor.

Lulu's first comment was, "I'm having a good day. The stitches are not at all bothering me."

Tanya confirmed this by saying, "We had a nice long walk this morning, the first one we've had in a week."

At the time, I was unaware that Lulu had just had her second operation, where she was given thirty-six stitches. She went on, "I hate going to the vet because they insist on shaving my belly. It really makes me feel bad. I don't like the razor they use."

Mom told me, "Yes, that's true. When I brought her back this last time, she had big razor burns. I don't know whether to put a cream on it or just let her rest instead."

By now, Tanya was convinced that we were indeed having a conversation with Lulu. I had already explained that when we have a good, deep dialogue, animals look as if they've fallen asleep when, in fact, they're in a deep state of meditation, focusing all their efforts on exchanging images with me.

Tanya had been watching Lulu, who had been chewing a bone and making quite a racket when I first closed my eyes, but was now silent. Because my eyes were closed, I didn't know that as soon as we'd started the session, Lulu had stopped chewing and laid on her side, eyes closed. Later, Tanya said, "I didn't believe you at first but, the moment you two started to talk, Lulu did exactly what you said she would."

More confident now, Tanya asked Lulu, "Why this disease?"

Death and Euthanasia, or "It's Okay to Cry"

Lulu was very specific. "For the longest time, breast cancer has been your obsession. It's always on your mind so I decided to become your teacher and show you how it appears, how it feels, what can be done about it, alternatives that are available, and finally how to leave this earth with dignity and understanding. It is what I mean to do and there's no turning back."

Tanya was speechless. Finally, she managed to ask, "How does Lulu know this? Indeed, breast cancer runs in my family, and it is my obsession, even as a young girl. I worry constantly about getting it and have a mammogram every year."

Lulu went on to explain, "I am your exact reflection and everything that goes on inside me reflects the way you feel, even think. Like the time we went to Arizona to visit some relatives, and I was stressed out because you were unhappy."

Tanya agreed. "Yes, I wasn't looking forward to my visit with those relatives and I was upset before the trip, during the ride, and all the

Lulu

The brave English Sheepdog is shown here after her surgery, which required thirty-six stitches.

time we were there. I was unhappy and restless, just like Lulu was. Tell me, is there any way I can help?"

Lulu told me, "Yes, tell her I am receptive to almost any kind of treatment that Tanya can think of as alternative medicine and will be very good about it. When the time comes, I want to experience the least amount of pain possible, being helped by painkilling drugs if necessary. When that's no longer feasible, I would like to go quickly. Meanwhile, can we spend as much time as possible together, doing things like walking and enjoying each other's company?"

Not long after our consultation, Tanya helped Lulu to make the transition. Tanya was lucky to have such a wonderful teacher and friend, and it made her decision to euthanize her much less painful, knowing that it was Lulu's choice.

In my talks, I am often asked, "When animals live with other animals, do they know when one of them gets sick?"

From what they tell me, all animals are aware when another is sick. If the sickness has been developing for a long time, animals will realize this before humans do. Often they leave the sick animal to itself and no longer request it to join in play. At other times, they will lie close to it to give it comfort and love. If the animal who is sick is the "top dog" of the house, he will, at some appropriate time, "pass the baton" to another, who will become "top dog" when the ill one is gone. I have seen this many times. The next story illustrates how it happens.

Spud

I was seeing Charlie and Sybil because, a week earlier, Charlie had lost the love of his life, a male fourteen-year-old Queensland heeler named Spud. He had been the first pet in the house and had been "top dog."

The couple still had two other dogs: another Queensland heeler, a nine-year-old female named Blue, and Toby, a ten-year-old schipperke male.

Before we started, Charlie was already highly emotional and I knew that I would fare no better once I made contact with Spud, so we grabbed two boxes of tissues and began. Spud came in immediately and told Charlie, "I'm feeling fine now and have been close to you all this time."

A tearful Charlie said, "Tell Spud that I know my love for him is holding him back."

Spud replied, "Yes, I know, but I'm in no hurry to leave. I can stay around for as long as need be. The only thing I'm concerned about is the fact Dad is in so much pain. I wish he could remember me without the heartache." (During our long conversation, he said this many times.)

Charlie said, "Could you ask him why it all happened so quickly? He seemed fine on the Saturday prior to his death, enjoying life so much and then, all of a sudden, he was diagnosed with a defective heart and died the next day."

Spud said, "I chose to go quickly to avoid so much grieving. You did nothing wrong. It was quick and almost without pain. I was able to enjoy my life right up to the very last minute. That was something worth living for."

Sybil, Charlie's wife, then said, "I had a vision of Spud trying to tell me something but I couldn't receive it. Could you please ask him what he was trying to say to me?"

Spud said, "I was trying to tell Sybil to help Dad through this hard time. It's difficult because there isn't much she can do. Dad is very much like a yo-yo. He seems to need her one moment, and the next, he needs his privacy. But try to help him as best you can. I assure you that I'm in no hurry to leave, and will always stay around you. I just wish that there'll be no more tears, only joy."

Death and Euthanasia, or "It's Okay to Cry"

Then, as if to lighten things up, he added, "I've given my 'top dog' job to Toby now, who is eager to talk."

Toby, the male schipperke, was a real talker and couldn't wait for his turn. He had come over to the couch at least three times while we were still talking with Spud and tried to interrupt by licking my face. Toby proudly boasted, "I've taken Spud's place. He and I often argued about who was top dog. Spud told me that now it's my turn."

When I relayed to Charlie and Sybil that Toby was in training for top dog, he showed me the pictures of him barking at the front door for strangers and something to do with horses, as if to reinforce the picture of him being top dog now. Sybil told me, "Just this morning, he moved his food bowl to where Spud's bowl used to be on the patio, and now he's sitting where Spud used to sit in the living room."

"Now that all of Spud's jobs are my responsibility, I'm trying to do good," Toby added.

When I asked Mom and Dad what Toby had been trying to do with horses (even though I had no idea they had horses), Dad explained, "We have a few horses outside and it was Spud's job to round them up at feeding time. As a Queensland heeler, herding was in his blood and he was very good at it. Toby, who stands only a few inches from the ground, on the other hand, doesn't have a clue. He just stands and barks at the horses, thinking that they will understand his command, which they ignore completely."

Mom asked, "Can you tell Toby not to get too close to the horses? I'm afraid he'll get stepped on or even kicked."

I explained to her, "Animals can't understand images to not do something. Can you give Toby a different job instead?"

She said, "How about taking care of the gophers on the property?"

Toby was very receptive. "I'd love another job. I like the gopher idea since I'm so much closer to the ground and it will be fun. Besides, I have a great sense of smell." (On a follow-up visit, they told me that

Toby had stopped bothering the horses and was doing a great job at getting the gopher population under control.)

Toby was doing exactly what Spud had been doing all those years. He had been given the go-ahead by the boss, who was now watching him from the other side.

If the grief of the preceding family was enormous, one can only imagine the grief of anyone faced with having to euthanize a loving pet. *Webster's New World Dictionary* gives the origin of the word *euthanasia* as the Greek words *eu,* meaning "well," and *thanatos,* meaning "death." So, literally, it means "good death." As meanings, the dictionary gives: (1) an easy and painless death; (2) the act or method of causing death painlessly to end suffering.

If there is one message that I get loud and clear every time I look into the eyes of dying pets, it is that they measure their happiness by the quality of their life. When it's time to go because of old age, incurable disease, injury, or serious behavioral problems, you are not depriving them of a good quality of life. In fact, you are a friend who is helping to ease their suffering and providing the inevitable passage. You are giving them the privilege of a good death and they regard that every bit as important as a good life.

Jessie

When Michelle called me in desperation one Saturday morning, I had no idea that Jessie, her cat and friend of many years, had been given three injections in a week to bring him, almost literally, back from the dead. When she called me, she said, "I must have a reading today and am willing to drive to you if you can fit me in."

I could not refuse, so we set up an afternoon appointment. An hour later, she called back. "I had to take Jessie to the emergency room because he was short of breath. He might not make it through the day, so can I come right now?"

Two hours later, Jessie, a male twelve-year-old brown tabby, Michelle, her husband, Tom, and I were talking while Michelle held Jessie on her lap. Jessie was doing better, but his eyes were yellow with jaundice and he remained very still and quiet. By now, Michelle knew in her heart that she would have to euthanize him, but she had a lot of questions for Jessie. She began by asking, "Will Jessie come back to me?"

When I asked him, Jessie said lovingly, "I still have a lot of things to teach her and without a doubt I will be coming back to her."

When she asked how she would know it was him, he answered, "I will make myself so irresistible to your eyes that you will have to take me home."

Then he added, "I was in charge of the household and have already 'passed the baton' onto Sinbad (a younger male at home). I spoke to all the other pets and am confident that the transition will be smooth."

Michelle confirmed that. "In the past week, Sinbad has been climbing onto our cat tree and taking the top ledge. I guess his position at the top represents his new status. Jessie always took that spot but he hasn't been able to climb up the tree. We have four other cats in the house, and I'm positive that Sinbad is now in charge. The change happened just as Jessie said. Can you ask him about the dog?"

Still with a spark of good humor left in him, Jessie said, "I don't want to talk about the dog. I don't particularly like him and always stay out of his way as much as I can."

Then I asked him the inevitable question: "Do you know you are dying?"

"Yes! Of course I do," Jessie said indignantly. "I have been ready to go for a while. In fact, this very morning I was ready to leave. And I'm ready right now! I would like you to help me go. It would be great if Dad could be with me, holding me. It would mean so much to me. I know how hard it would be for Mom to be there, and that's why I am

67

not asking her. I know she could not handle it. She needs to understand, though, that I am ready to leave, that my body can't take it anymore."

When I relayed this, Michelle began crying but managed to say to Jessie, "If you really want me to be there, I will, even though it will feel as if someone is ripping my heart out."

Jessie thanked her, but said, "I know how you feel and offering to be there means a lot to me. As long as Dad is there, there'll be someone I'm comfortable with in the room and I'll be okay. Please don't worry so much."

We all cried like babies. Here was brave Jessie at the end of his life, and still comforting his mom! The pain of letting go is so contagious, yet I was elated to learn from this wise animal that my tears of sorrow were mixed with those of love and understanding.

"It's okay to cry," I reminded them, reaching for another tissue.

About a week later I received a beautiful card bearing a picture of a short-haired, brown tabby kitten with bright blue eyes drinking milk out of a teacup, milk dripping down his lower lip. Inside, the note read:

> Dear Monica,
>
> Thank you for seeing us on such short notice last Saturday, and accommodating your schedule to us. It was such a blessing that we were able to speak to Jessie in the last few hours of his life through your gift. The gratitude we feel is immeasurable. We will always remember the peaceful, courageous, and dignified way Jessie left this world.
>
> We are so grateful for the time we spent with you. You gave Jessie a voice that we hold in our hearts. You helped answer some difficult questions that enabled us to let him go with acceptance and serenity.
>
> Sincerely,
>
> Michelle and Tom

On the death of an animal in a multi-pet household, try to allow the remaining animals to see and smell the body of the deceased one so that there can be no doubt. And if you must unavoidably have a pet euthanized, send images to the remaining animals of what will happen at the vet's office. Picture the animal's body going limp as the spirit rises from it. This may sound morbid but, I assure you, animals are far more accepting of death than we are, as many of my stories reveal.

Many of my human clients are less ready than their animals to face the inevitable, and will try different avenues to avert or delay death, as in this next story of courage and determination.

Blue Boy

A few weeks earlier, I had seen Blue Boy when Mary had called me in for a consultation. Pete and Mary had been gone on a ten-day vacation and, on their return, they found Blue Boy had been scratching and pulling the fur under his chin. Thinking it was stress related, they'd called to set up an appointment for me to see him.

When I saw the raw spot under his chin, I knew that it wasn't stress and asked them to take Blue Boy immediately to a holistic vet I knew. I was confident that with a few changes in his diet, he would soon be okay. We went ahead and held the session anyway since I was already there, and I was pleased to get to know Blue Boy a little better. He was a great cat, polite and friendly.

He was also quite intelligent and surprised us all by trying to figure out the cause of his allergic reaction. I asked Mary and Pete whether any new fragrances, detergents, soaps, hair sprays, colognes, candles, or perfumes had been introduced to the household lately. The answer was no. We also went through clothing, blankets, carpet cleaners, kitchen disinfectants, and the like. Nothing.

With my eyes closed, I told them, "Blue Boy is taking me on a pictorial tour of the house. [I had not had the usual tour of the actual house.] He's stopped in a bedroom upstairs and is looking up in front of him. I see a figure of a human, not very distinct, but I know this person is doing something there. Blue Boy is showing me someone ironing. Mary, do you use the spare bedroom upstairs to iron in?"

Mary replied, "No. I always iron downstairs."

"Well, Blue Boy insists that it's something about the iron. Do you do any crafts up there?"

"Pete puts together model airplanes up there."

I was excited to hear this because I knew the glue or the metallic paint could be very toxic to cats, but Pete said, "My models don't require paint. They come pre-painted and all I have to do is iron them to shrink them to size."

We all got it at the same time. Ironing in the spare bedroom! None of us could believe Blue Boy had told us about that. I don't know if the ironing of plastic gave off certain toxic fumes or not because we never did find the exact cause of his allergy. But with a change in diet, Blue Boy was soon back to his old self. That's why I was puzzled when Pete left a message on my machine a couple of weeks later requesting another reading, saying, "Blue Boy is very ill."

Due to my busy schedule, we couldn't make a date until the following Wednesday, a week away. When I arrived, Blue Boy lay in the corner of the living room surrounded by blankets and towels so he could pick the best spot. Food and water dishes and two litter boxes were close by. He greeted me by smelling my hand and allowing me to touch his forehead. He twitched the tip of his tail in response.

Mary and Pete anxiously told me, "He's not eating and refuses any kind of food offered. We're force-feeding him three times a day and injecting water under his skin because he is so dehydrated. We found him hiding under the couch two days ago and today he was asleep in the litter box we keep down the hall, in the spare bedroom. It seemed as if he expended all his energy to get to the box he usually uses and then didn't have the strength to return to the living room, so he just stayed inside the box and fell asleep, exhausted. All this is very strange for

Death and Euthanasia, or "It's Okay to Cry"

him. The vet diagnosed him with some kidney failure but is still running tests. Our next appointment is in two days."

With a heavy heart, I told Pete and Mary, "Based on my experience, I think Blue Boy is near his end, and his behaviors are signs he's giving that say, 'I'm ready to go now.'"

Pete refused to just give up and stop force-feeding him. "I just can't do it. Can you somehow convince him that, even though he might not be feeling good now, modern medicine might have a cure? I want him to give me a few more days. We need time to get the test results back and then for some kind of medication to work. We'll do whatever it takes, and will not give up the fight."

I couldn't argue with Pete's sentiment and turned to Blue Boy. The first thing he said was, "I've stuck around because Mom and Dad didn't want me to go. I know I'm loved and my home has been a good one. But I really am ready to go now."

When I relayed that to Pete, he begged, "Just give us a little longer, Blue Boy."

Reluctantly and after much convincing, Blue Boy said, "Okay, I'll give you no more than a week."

Pete said, "Thank you. If you're not better in a week, we can talk about it then. But I'm sure you will see some improvement."

Our conversation continued with many important questions. When we talked about how his illness felt, Blue Boy described his feelings by sending me the pain and where it was concentrated. When he showed me how his mouth felt puffy, I suddenly had difficulty talking, for my lips kept sticking to my teeth. As he talked about how swollen his throat felt and how hard breathing was, my chest began to hurt, and my heart began beating very fast, especially every time I moved. He shared the feeling of being force-fed, and the food made my stomach turn. I gagged and could not even swallow water. My body was cold all over and I was trembling and shivering uncontrollably. The constant pain made me miserable.

As I described all this to Mary, she said, "I love Blue Boy too much to put him through this. I can't ask him to suffer this much just because of our grief. Will you tell Blue Boy that I release him to go whenever he feels he can no longer stand the pain?"

After a long silence, Blue Boy finally answered, "That is the best gift you could give me."

He then reminded his tearful dad of how close they'd been. "You learned how to love a kitten, understand an adolescent, and be friends with an adult. We have a very deep understanding of each other and you will be loved forever."

To Mary, he said, "You're the tough one in the family, the one who set up the rules. I didn't mind your rules and thought they were proper. I know I can count on your strength now. You know I always tried to be the perfect gentleman."

Mary replied, "I always told you that you were."

He went on to warn his humans what to expect during his final moments and what to do. "Please stay calm and don't pick me up to cuddle me. My breath will become labored until I can't breathe anymore. That is the way things should be."

Faced with this cat's incredible courage, we all cried for an hour and I left exhausted. As I did, I said, "Yes, Mary. It's okay to cry."

As I fell asleep that night, my last thought of the day went to Blue Boy, how he had bravely agreed to put up with another week of intense pain and discomfort to please his dad, and how relieved he'd been when his mom had released him.

The next morning, I received an e-mail:

Dear Family and Friends,

A few of you know that in the past two weeks, our beloved cat, Blue Boy, became quite ill—kidney failure and some other factor that his doctors were unable to pinpoint. Pete and I rode a roller coaster of hope and despair as we struggled with Bluey's process.

The roller coaster stopped last night—about 9:45 PM on November 8—as Bluey made his final transition. We had received information as to how the end would look, and were able to be calm and supportive in his last minutes. For this gift, we are immeasurably grateful. Bluey, always a generous spirit, made things as easy for us as he could.

We are also full of gratitude to all of you who have extended your loving thoughts to the three of us in recent days, and we know that so many more of you would have done so if we had only let you know. So, we appreciate your continued support as Pete and I come to terms with the large hole in our hearts in the days to come. If we seem a little far away at times, you can guess the reason; release and acceptance do not come all at once.

Bluey gave us so many gifts during his eleven years with us, and one of the final ones was a truer understanding of the depth of the love that Pete and I share, and of how grateful we are for all of the wonderful, supportive people in our lives, many of whom are receiving this e-mail today. Thank you. We love you so very much.

—Mary and Pete

> *Blue Boy*
> *In our lives, 1989 to 2000*
> *In our hearts, forever.*

The next e-mail was addressed personally to me:

Dear Monica,

We are thankful for your help in our last evening with Blue Boy. The following words in our previous message were meant for you:

"We had received information as to how the end would look, and were able to be calm and supportive in his last minutes.

For this gift we are immeasurably grateful. Bluey, always a generous spirit, made things as easy for us as he could."

Bluey left exactly as he told us he would through you, just two hours earlier.

Pete and I felt closure after our session together, so when Bluey left physical form so soon afterward, we were guided and comforted by what we had learned. We were also very grateful that we had released him from his promise and said that it was okay with us for him to go when he had to, if he couldn't hold out.

Blue Boy

He waited until his humans told him it was okay to go.

Thank you again so much for sharing your gift with us. We will be recommending you to others, and calling you again when we bring another spirit in animal form into our household.

Peace be with you, and with all of us.

Blue Boy's story stresses how important it is for us to convey our acceptance of our pets' final wishes and allow them to make their transition on their terms and in their own time.

Bailey

When a friend dies, our expression of love is no less if it is not seen outwardly; on the inside, we still feel the void.

I recently received an e-mail about a dog killed in a traffic accident that his two brothers might have witnessed. Dee, their guardian, explained that her sister, while visiting her home, had by mistake left the garage door open and all three dogs had decided to take an adventure around the neighborhood. Katie and Emmitt came back; Bailey didn't. When the whole family went looking for him, they found him dead by the roadside, the casualty of a busy street.

Devastated, guilt-ridden, and upset, they called me in for closure. Bailey, in his unique style, made sure to tell the person who'd left the garage door open that it wasn't her fault. He made it very clear that nobody was to blame. I had no idea at the time what he was talking about, but Dee understood and explained briefly that her sister had been moving some things into the garage and walked into the house without realizing that the door connecting the garage to the kitchen was also open. The dogs, usually kept inside the house, were then free to get out.

Through me, Dee asked the other two dogs what they remembered, but they had both run ahead and were not with Bailey at the time of the accident. They added that they both missed Bailey very much.

75

As our conversation continued, Dee was able to tell Bailey many things that she'd never expressed before. Maybe because of this "opening up" of feelings, she decided to write it all down. Dee kindly allowed me to include her poem in an effort to help people cope with their feelings.

In Memory of Bailey

I never really wanted three dogs;
Two was quite enough,
But then sweet Bailey crossed my path
And my heart was filled with love.

He'd had a rough beginning
And was constantly timid and scared,
But with time he came to trust again
And his broken heart repaired.

He had so much love to give;
He lived for his next hug.
Katie and Emmitt were his best friends
And he loved just being loved.

Bailey held a special place
In my heart of hearts,
A dog that had been so very hurt
But had come so very far.

Each night that I laid down in bed
Bailey was right by my side.
He'd have me hold his paws till he fell asleep
And then he'd be all right.

Death and Euthanasia, or "It's Okay to Cry"

He loved to play with the other dogs
But now he is at rest.
And how we'll manage without him here
Is really anybody's guess.

I'll miss his black nose and ears
With his white paws and belly,
And him lying in his favorite spot
And even when he'd roll in something smelly.

I'll miss his excited bark
When I'd come home to see them;
In his eyes I could do no wrong
And that is quite a feeling.

He loved to go for rides
Out the window he'd hang his head.
And feeding him scraps under the table
Was a bad habit I'll never regret.

He'd lick my tears when I would cry,
Closer than any trusted friend.
And he loved me unconditionally
Right up until the end.

So now our family is a little smaller
Although our hearts have grown
Because of this dog that loved us so much
And just wanted a home of his own.

Death and Euthanasia, or "It's Okay to Cry"

No words can truly express
The loss I feel inside,
For such a sweet and innocent soul
A million tears are left to cry.

I hope Bailey knew how much we love him
And how we didn't want him to leave.
But we know he had to travel on
Yet our hearts are left to grieve.

There's an empty spot on the couch now
Where he always used to lay.
And the other dogs haven't been hungry
And neither wants to play.

We will miss you, Bailey,
In so very many ways.
You were such a special boy
And nothing will be quite the same.

I know he is in Heaven now
A home far better than this.
And if anyone can love him as much as we did
His name would be Jesus.

So this I pray, dear Lord,
Heal his wounds and scars.
Make him whole and healthy again
And keep him in your arms.

Death and Euthanasia, or "It's Okay to Cry"

Tell him that I love him
And Katie and Emmitt, too.
And remind him that we miss him
I put my trust in you.

And one more thing I pray
Please keep my faithful friend
In your loving, caring home
Until we can all be a family again.

All of our love,
Mom, Katie, Emmitt & Julie

Death and Euthanasia, or "It's Okay to Cry"

CHAPTER 6

Is Beauty In the Eye of the Beholder?

In his book *All My Patients Are Under the Bed*, veterinarian Dr. Louis J. Camuti jokes that most of his patients hide from him in anticipation of his visit. By age eighty-five, he had a lot of experience with felines and could second-guess them every time by being the fastest shot in the East (vaccinating them very quickly during office visits). However, on home visits, the cats knew that he was coming, so would always hide under the bed.

Because of this and because I like to plan ahead, I make a conscious effort to "talk" to my clients before I go to their homes. Many times my appointments are in the evening when the humans return home from work, so in the morning I spend time "calling on" the animals and explaining that I am coming to talk to them, that it will be their chance to tell their side of the story and, best of all, their chance to request any changes to be made in their lives.

After this "softening up," dogs and many cats usually greet me eagerly at the door. Some will come to see me and then respectfully hide under the dinette table or behind the couch, but they are there to say hi. Some are just curious; others want to talk immediately. All of them are open-minded, even the shy ones.

The first story features one of the most outgoing cats I have ever had the opportunity to meet.

Sierra

Wendy called me in to talk to her two girls: Sierra, a chocolate point Siamese, and Sapphire, a lilac point. One of them had not been using the litter box and Wendy was at her wit's end. She wanted to know which cat was the culprit and what to do about it. I was a referral from one of her friends and, as Wendy herself put it, her last resort. Skeptical of psychic abilities and New Age thinking, she'd heard of telepathy but had never given it much thought. When her friend had told her about me, she'd laughed but reasoned that it couldn't hurt since nothing else was working.

As Wendy and I walked from the main gate of the condo complex to her condo, she joked, "The girls will probably be hiding under the bed."

Knowing better, I chuckled under my breath.

When she opened the door, Sierra, the older girl, was perched high on the arm of the couch waiting for me and, as any respectful Siamese would do, greeted me with a loud meow.

I immediately marveled at her beautiful markings and told her, "You are extremely beautiful and I am proud to make your acquaintance."

Deciding that I must be okay, she let me pet her.

Wendy's home was small but cozy. Just to the right of the dinette table and against the wall was a covered litter box with litter splatter all around the entrance.

Wendy took me to one of the bedrooms to see where one of the cats had had an "accident" on top of the bedspread, the main reason I was there.

Returning to the living room, I sat down on the couch and Sierra sat next to me, eager to talk. She kept rubbing her body against me and meowing to get my attention. As soon as I made contact, Sierra said, "Tell Wendy to show you my picture. I used to be more beautiful than I am now and I want you to see the picture to show you exactly how beautiful I really was."

Wendy said, "I have some pictures of Sierra, but can't recall offhand exactly where they are. I'll look before you leave. They must be somewhere in the house."

Sierra was about eleven years old and had gained a lot of weight in the last few years. Although her belly had gotten big and was hanging down, almost touching the floor, she still moved with grace and form. Using a series of images, Sierra confessed, "Tell Mom that it's me who doesn't use the litter box all the time. It's covered, which I don't like. I can't fit in the opening since my tummy rubs the bottom of the pan and hurts me. The big litter pieces are hard on my feet and my beautiful fur gets soiled and I have to spend a lot of time cleaning myself since the box is so dirty."

She also complained about her sister. "Sapphire, who is so prim and proper, and I are always fighting for Mom's attention."

Is Beauty In the Eye of the Beholder?

I relayed all this to Wendy, and added, "You have to look for a bigger box without a top, change the litter to a finer grain or softer texture, and promise to keep the box clean."

Wendy sighed, reluctantly agreeing that she was part of the problem, and promised to change her cleaning habits.

I imaged that to Sierra, who then complained that she could not go outside. "I love the sun and the green. I am a nature girl, just like Mom, and love to be outdoors."

Wendy was surprised at this and acknowledged that she was indeed a nature girl, spending all of her vacations in nature. Wendy told Sierra, "It's dangerous for you to be let outside. It's a busy street."

Sierra suggested, "Can I play on the balcony where there are a lot of nice plants?"

Wendy agreed that it would be okay and also suggested that she could walk with Sierra on the grounds of the complex, as long as Sierra promised to stay close. They both happily agreed to try it.

When I made contact with nine-year-old Sapphire, Wendy asked her about the gray male cat that makes the rounds of the complex and visits the girls. "Since both girls are spayed now, I let him in. Sierra likes him very much and they spend some time together playing, but Sapphire spits and hisses at him, and tries to slap him. Has the cat done anything wrong? What's her problem?"

Sapphire told me, "I had a traumatic experience with a boy when I was supposed to be bred and, from that day, I wanted nothing at all to do with boys. They're trouble. They're mean bullies and I just don't want anything to do with them. Ask Mom not to let him in."

Wendy was shocked at this and explained, "Many years ago, I took Sapphire to a stud service. Since Sapphire was so special, I wanted her to have pretty kittens, too, so I contacted the best breeder I could find and drove for an hour and a half with Sapphire to meet the little prince. I knew right away that it wasn't a good match. Sapphire was not happy with her beau, but he was quite eager. The breeder told me, 'Don't worry. I can make Sapphire get pregnant by holding her down while the tom performs his duty. It's quite common. Everybody does it.'

"Well, I drove back home with a heavy heart. I just couldn't get the pleading in Sapphire's eyes out of my mind and the look on her face when I left her at the house. Back home, I called the breeder to tell him I'd changed my mind and was coming back to get my cat. I drove all the way back, and poor Sapphire was so traumatized that she spent the next week hiding from me, barely eating and showing no sign of love or affection.

"I knew that Sapphire was upset about that day, but had no idea it would last for years and make her hate every single tom that crosses her path."

This was an important lesson for Wendy, and a communication that she would not soon forget.

After my contact with Sapphire, Sierra reminded me to tell Wendy to show me the picture. She went off to look and returned with a large frame with places to hold photos in a collage. She handed it to me, pointing to the lower right corner that showed the two girls embracing each other. Sierra, who was still sitting to my left on the couch, indignantly told me, "*No, that's not the one!*" Then she pawed at the frame to call my attention.

In the upper left of the frame, I saw the photo that I immediately recognized as the one Sierra mentally sent (see photographs, page 86). Excitedly I called to Wendy, who had left to look for more pictures. Wendy told me, "Wow, I'd completely forgot about that picture. A professional photographer took it at one of the cat shows where Sierra won a first place championship."

No wonder Sierra wanted me to see that photo. I could see why she was so proud of it. She sat on a dark green blanket that accentuated her natural tan color. She looked royal indeed, with the air of elegance that only Siamese cats can have. Her light blue eyes shone and she looked over her left shoulder, her face slightly tilted.

Sierra and Sapphire

The top photo is of Sierra in her beauty queen days; the bottom photo shows the two sisters, Sierra and Sapphire, snuggling.

Is Beauty In the Eye of the Beholder?

"That's the one," Sierra said proudly. "Now that is what being beautiful is all about."

She was proud of winning first place and wanted me to see what a real beauty looked like. I had to agree that she had been one great-looking cat. But you are still a beautiful cat, Sierra, inside and out, and I am proud to have met you.

About a week later, Wendy wrote me an e-mail:

> Hi there!
>
> I was just e-mailing Millie (a friend) back and forth, and she really wants you to see the e-mail I sent her regarding your visit! I really like your website, by the way, and my friend and I will be at your Saturday workshop to learn how to talk to our cats!
>
> Thanks again!
>
> Wendy
>
>
> Hi Millie:
>
> You wouldn't believe how Tuesday night went with Dr. Monica. At first she was talking to Sierra. She told me things and I almost had to laugh, but I would write them down, just so I'd remember later how funny this all seemed. But I tried a few things she recommended, and WHAM! Sierra's now using the litter box again. I've got to see if I can find the wheat litter, but they're not jealous of each other anymore. I can spend time with one and not have the other coming over to fight. She said they had a lot to say to me and thanked me for bringing her over.
>
> Turns out Sierra's a nature girl, just like me. I wish I was going to be home this weekend to see how she develops/re-acts to other things I learned about her.

And Sapphire hates anything to do with males because of when I tried to breed her with that Grand Champion stud. I knew when I left there, I felt uncomfortable. I called as soon as I got home, and the guy said you'd better come get your cat, nothing's gonna happen here. So I did. She was so scared and coiled up, just like when I got her. Sapphire said when she first met me, we made a pact together that she knew she could trust me and that I'd take care of her.

She purred on my shoulder from minute one. Definitely want to learn how to talk to them myself, seems so fascinating.

—Wendy

It seems that Wendy's initial skepticism had disappeared, along with Sierra's little "quirk." As a result of this consultation and my workshop on animal communication, Wendy changed her mind about the possibilities of being able to speak with her cats. To this date, she tries to maintain a dialog with them and doesn't even mind when her roommate scoffs at her!

Kahn

Kahn is a male Persian who lives in Korea with his human mom and his twenty-one siblings. Yes, twenty-one!

I get calls from all over the world, so to speak with an animal in another country is not unusual for me. What was unusual was the fact that a producer from a Korean television program called me to do an interview and then to have a consultation with a couple of animals. To do this I had to be ready at 4 PM—because of the change of hours, it would be 9 AM in Korea the next morning. I also had the producer next to me because the owner of the cat did not speak English.

I don't have a language problem with the animals since they speak in picture telepathy. Therefore I can communicate at any time with anyone in the world.

When I established communication with Kahn, he immediately told me that he was beautiful, and he was proud of his looks and his long, beautiful fur. But he was livid! His mom had cut his hair short and now he felt terrible. To be able to explain himself and to give his mom clues, he had been urinating all over the house and getting into fights with his siblings. Because he was considerably smaller in stature, he had to get rid of his frustration by attacking only the females who were smaller than him, even with his new haircut, and of course all the kittens were getting the brunt of his rage.

Kahn was so upset that he demanded to be taken away and given a new set of human parents with no siblings. Mom was heartbroken and said to ask him what she could do to make him feel better.

As gently as I could, I told Kahn that this behavior needed to stop, but he wouldn't hear my request. He told me that he would stop when his hair grew back and not before. He made his mom promise never, ever to cut his hair again.

Through the translator, his mom was shaken. She told us she had taken Kahn to have his hair shaved and had noticed a change in attitude right away but she didn't realize that was the reason why. She was crying and promised Kahn never to cut his hair again.

In the meantime, poor Kahn will have to be separated from all his siblings until such time when he can, once again, hold his head up high and know he is the most beautiful cat on his turf!

CHAPTER 7

Lost Pets

As an animal communicator, I find locating lost pets to be extremely challenging and often decline the request. Pinpointing a location is difficult when I can only go on what the animal can see and hear.

Tinker

"My cat Tinker has been missing for two days. Can you please help me?"

I vividly remember that phone call from Vickie; I told her that I would do what I could. When I got in contact with Tinker, I saw what she was seeing through a crack in whatever was in front of her. I saw mud, and sensed that she was lonely, cold, wet, and in some place dark. Then I saw a woman who Tinker could see through the crack. She was tall, slim, with blond hair down to her shoulders. She wore brown shoes and a skirt that came down to just above her knees. She was walking slowly and whistling.

"You just described me perfectly," Vickie said excitedly. "I came home from work and went immediately looking for Tinker in our neighborhood. There's a new house under construction just across the street from me and, because of all the rain, there's a lot of mud where the lawn will be. I bet she's trapped somewhere over there."

Three days later, Vickie called back. "I had no luck finding my lovely Tinker. Could you try again?"

Reluctantly, I tried to go back to the last picture from three days earlier. I was back inside the dark place and could see the crack in front of me. I saw daylight but this time it was different. I knew I was alone and not watching through the cat's eyes. I moved my point-of-view outside and saw how the mud was drying in some places but was still soft. I turned around and saw pieces of wood and sawdust, but still no sign of Tinker. I went out into the street and did a complete 360-degree scan while calling out Tinker's name and asking—no, pleading—for her to answer. I tried to make contact, but couldn't. Tinker was unable to send me any more information or pictures. She was gone.

Passing on heart-breaking news such as this is the most distressing part of my work, but not all lost pet cases end so tragically, as in the next story.

The Shih Tzu

One day I got a desperate phone call from a woman in tears. Between sobs, she told me, "My granddaughter's Shih Tzu was abducted from the front lawn of my house a few hours ago. Can you find out where he is?"

The little dog, although still a puppy, was able to tell me that he was with a family with a child, probably a boy, since I could see the hair was quite short. I could see a mom fussing over the dog and also a man in the background who was uninvolved in whatever the mother and son were doing. The boy was playing with the little dog, who was not scared.

When I asked the dog how he'd gotten there, he said, "I was walking in front of my mom's house and then got sidetracked. I went to visit the man next door who was working in the garage. I was taken from the neighbor's house on a short car ride over to where I am now."

Armed with that information, Grandma thought she knew where to start asking questions.

The granddaughter called me back the next day and told me, "Based on your description of events and places, we were able to find out where the puppy was taken. Our neighbors, a mother and son, thought the puppy was a stray and took him to the home of her other son, just a few minutes away. This man has a little boy and they thought the dog would be happy there."

I always worry about giving people false hopes in cases such as this, but this time I was absolutely sure about the information coming in and the outcome.

Spike

Some time ago, I had consulted for the Smith family and their three dogs, including Spike, a three-year-old male boxer. Mr. and Mrs. Smith and three of their children had looked on in amazement while the communication was taking place. I was pleased to see a new understanding forming in the minds of those three teenagers, who obviously loved and cherished their pets.

Ricky (Mrs. Smith) called me late one evening to tell me, "My oldest son, John, took Spike with him Saturday on a trip to Victorville (a few hours away) to visit with some friends. The friends have a large backyard and John thought nothing about leaving Spike there while he was inside the house with his friends. Besides, sometimes he likes it outside because it's cooler. Well, on Sunday morning when John went outside to feed Spike, he was nowhere to be found. Frantic, they combed the neighborhood all day without success. Hoping he would find Spike and not have to upset us, John waited to call us with the news, but then tired, full of guilt, and shaken, he finally called me on Sunday evening to tell me he was coming home without Spike."

Ricky, a very strong and willful woman, and very much the drill sergeant of the family, told John in no uncertain terms that he was not allowed to come back home without Spike. She then went into action. First thing Monday morning, she called the animal shelter in the area and also those in surrounding counties. Then she made over a thousand flyers including Spike's picture and her many phone numbers. She called all the veterinarians and vet hospitals in the area with a description of Spike and left numbers as well. She asked John and his friends to canvass the whole area again . . . and again. Finally, she planned to take Jasmine, her female boxer and the love of Spike's life, all the way to Victorville. She figured that if Spike was aimlessly wandering, Jasmine could urinate to mark the area and give Spike a smell that he would recognize.

Leaving no stone unturned, Ricky also called me for help and advice. I knew Spike well from our previous conversations and contacted him easily. I told him, "Your family loves you and wants you back. A lot of people are looking for you."

He replied, "I'm scared. I've lost my sense of smell and can't recognize anything. I don't know which way I should be going."

I tried to send him a picture of the house where he had stayed with John and asked him to go back there. "John is too busy to care for me so I'm not going back there," he said.

The conversation went back and forth for a while and I finally asked Spike to remain where he was and not to go anywhere. In the meantime, Ricky was getting ready to take Jasmine to Victorville Tuesday morning. However, she returned Wednesday with no Spike, no news, and no hope.

Six days had gone by since Spike had disappeared and I suddenly had a picture coming through from him, without me attempting to communicate. He showed me an image of a house near where he was hiding. I immediately called Ricky but she was again in Victorville, so I told her husband, "Spike is still there. He's hiding, which is why they can't find him. I asked him to show himself to the lady of the house that he is showing me in his picture. She will be able to help. He told me that he's cold since it's been raining the past two days. He is tired and very, very hungry. He is not sure if he can do what I ask. I told him how important it is for him just to be seen. The woman in that house needs to see him up close so that she can recognize him. I told him it's very important and everything will be okay if he can do that."

I added, "It's imperative that you do not give up the search. Spike is out there and will try to make himself be seen. Do not give up on him!"

Ricky had been searching for Spike for days and was exhausted. She had forsaken work, obligations, and family, refusing to give up the search. She had received dozens of phone calls in response to the flyers she had distributed but none was a good lead. Some people couldn't tell a boxer from a German shepherd and she'd been sent on one wild goose chase after another, which had slowed her down.

On Saturday afternoon, heartbroken, she decided to return home. Her daughter and youngest son had joined her, and all three were silent and tearful on the ride back, deep in their own thoughts and regrets, thinking about the good times they'd had with Spike and the tragedy of losing him.

Almost home, Ricky's beeper went off. The number on the screen showed a Victorville area code so they raced to the next exit, found a phone, and called the number. A woman on the other end described Spike perfectly. When she gave her address, Ricky realized that the woman's house was only two blocks away from where Spike had been staying. The woman went on to explain, "I've been trying to get the dog to come closer by enticing him with food but he only makes it so far and then turns around and is gone. I know he must be hungry because I can see his ribs sticking out."

Ricky and her kids spun around and headed back up to Victorville and the address the woman had given them. They immediately began searching the area, but Spike was nowhere to be found.

Undaunted, Ricky began to drive up and down every street with the car windows rolled down, as all three of them yelled, "Spike, Spike, Spike," and looked out in different directions. Dusk was approaching and they were exhausted, but the knowledge that he was close by spurred them on.

About a block away from where they'd started, Ricky noticed out of the corner of her eye something moving. She turned to look, but saw nothing. Wondering if it had been a trick of the light, she stopped the car and called Spike's name again, this time louder and with intention, as if to demand obedience.

Ricky's heart raced. Something was out there, for it moved again. In the gathering dusk, she saw a four-legged form. Again, another yell: "SPIKE!" The creature emerged from the shadows and began coming closer. "Yes, there he is. It's Spike, Spike, come here, boy! Oh, Spike, I love you so much. Where have you been?" Ricky cried, overjoyed.

As all three petted and fussed over him, Spike, the dog without a tail, couldn't move his rear end fast enough to express his love and appreciation. Ricky, on the other hand, knew exactly how to show Spike her love. The next stop was Burger King, where he got ten hamburgers, followed by a long sleep on the daughter's lap for the ride home.

I meet many people who are skeptical and do not believe in what I do or say. But most of them are open-minded enough to listen to what I see in the images animals send me. At no other time is this more true than at a time of distress, such as when one of their beloved pets is missing or presumed dead. As their last resort, even skeptics call me, sometimes expecting nothing other than reassurance. Others are unwilling to let any ray of hope slip by, as in the next case.

Sparky

Eileen called me to ask if I could talk to her two yellow labs regarding the disappearance of a third one. I thought this was an odd request and asked, "How come you want me to ask the other two?"

She replied, "They will know."

She wouldn't say any more so we made an appointment. She lived far away from me, but offered to drive with her two dogs to see me instead of waiting for me to have time to drive to her.

When she arrived, Eileen turned out to be in her mid-forties and I could tell she was in a lot of pain. With her were her daughter and two

97

female yellow Labradors, Hailey, four years old, and Kelly, seven. The missing dog, Sparky, was a 12½-year-old female.

Eileen must have done this before, I thought to myself, because she brought pictures of Sparky, her food dish, two stuffed toys, and her collar. But unlike most of my clients who love to talk about their pets and the specifics of their consultation, she remained quiet and expressionless.

"Before we begin," I asked, "Could you describe the outside of your house and what happened the night Sparky disappeared?"

Eileen was reluctant to talk, not wanting to reveal anything that I could somehow use in the reading. I understood perfectly and told her, "I need just a little information to be able to place the pictures I will be getting in the right context."

Eileen said, "That evening, I left the house twenty minutes before eight and came back home at eleven-fifteen. The front door was wide open. Sparky was missing and the other two dogs were inside the house. The house is located halfway down the street and has a driveway into the garage that is connected to the house."

Then she sat back and waited for me to start. Hailey said right away, "Sparky knows him, Sparky knows him. So she went with him."

Hailey then described from her viewpoint what she had seen. I relayed to Eileen and her daughter a description of the man I was seeing in Hailey's image. "He's wearing blue jeans, with a white shirt and a baseball cap. I can see that the legs are muscular and he's tan, like someone who works outside, and is very athletic. Hailey is also showing me a dark-colored pickup truck with something in the back."

Kelly interrupted us and said excitedly many times, "She knows him, she knows him."

Through me, Eileen asked the dogs, "Who took the stuffed toys outside?"

Kelly told her, "Sparky took one of them and I took the other. When Sparky dropped hers, I did the same. I saw Sparky going to the back of the truck and then it began to drive off. I decided to follow but was told, 'Stay!' I saw the truck leaving and wondered where Sparky was. When I realized that Sparky was not there, I heard Hailey calling me to come inside the house, so I turned around and went inside the house to be with her."

Mom then asked, "Was the front door broken?"

"No, it was a loud noise but it wasn't broken or forced."

"Can you describe the person?"

Kelly replied, "He was wearing a dark baseball cap. He looked like he was always outdoors, and doing some kind of exercise. He was a big man. The type of man that would love a big dog."

"Why didn't you go in the truck?" I asked.

"I wanted to go but he told us to stay. Why couldn't I go with Sparky? I was confused. We always go together. Why not this time? I've been very upset lately, not myself, especially in front of the door. It feels bad there."

Hailey added, "I was afraid and went back into the house. The house was a safe place to be. I told Kelly this."

Eileen said, "I have a photo. Could you try to tell from the picture if this is the same man that Hailey and Kelly are talking about?"

"I've never done that before but I'll give it a try," I said.

I opened my eyes and Eileen's daughter handed me the photo. I'd barely glanced at it when my eyes blurred with tears and my voice quivered. I said, "This is the absolute duplicate of the man I just saw in my mind. Unbelievable as it sounds, it's the honest-to-goodness truth."

Eileen relaxed now that she had her answer and explained things. "The photo is of my ex-husband. I think he's taken Sparky out of revenge. Sparky is my dog, while the other two belong to different family members. He's a building contractor and is outside on sites most of the day. He always wears blue jeans and is a big, muscular man. He's threatened to take Sparky away from me many, many times before.

99

"Sparky is very defensive of her home and surroundings, and she would never allow a stranger to open the door or come in the house without attacking that person. Also she would never take her toy outside the home for a stranger. I'm sure that Sparky would only take it out to play with someone she knew. That piece of information makes me sure that what I fear most is what's happened."

Eileen and I both became emotional and had to stop for a few seconds while we composed ourselves. She then asked me, "Can you try to contact Sparky directly from one of the photos I brought?"

When I did, Sparky told me, "I was put in the back of the truck and was very surprised because I used to always ride in the cab. The ride was long and it was very dark and I couldn't see anything except that, after a while, I could see a lot of light coming from the right."

She showed me images that looked as if they were on the freeway next to a big shopping mall.

Eileen exclaimed, "I know exactly where that is. My ex-husband has some friends about two hours away and I wouldn't be at all surprised if he's taken Sparky to them."

Sparky continued, "I saw a horse and other animals that were new to me. I have to sleep outside in a barn and that isn't right. But I'm being fed well and have lots of room to run and play during the day. I think it's odd that I can't go back home."

Sparky wasn't really questioning the change. I got the feeling that since her dad had taken her there, then she thought it must be okay.

Eileen then said, "We live in a very small town where everyone knows everybody. The police are out looking for Sparky every day. I've posted signs offering a thousand-dollar reward to anyone who finds her. I figure the only reason nobody has seen her in ten days is because she's not around."

Sadly, when Eileen confronted her ex-husband, he denied having anything to do with the incident, and she never saw Sparky again.

Lost Pets

Three months later, Eileen called to tell me, "One evening while preparing dinner, I felt one of my dogs bumping against the back of my knees like they always do but more forcefully. I ignored it but, five minutes later, it happened again even harder. When I turned round, though, neither of the girls was there. Curious as to how they could have gone out of the kitchen so fast, I went looking for them. I found both of them fast asleep on the living room floor. I was perplexed. Who or what touched me? It was so real! Was it some kind of sign? Do I need to be aware of something? You're the only person I could think of to ask."

I told her, "Based on my experience, this was probably Sparky saying goodbye, or hello, depending on which way you look at it. Sparky has made the transition to the other side and was visiting you to let you know how much she loves you."

That was the last time that Eileen felt Sparky. She has now moved on with her life, but Sparky will forever have a special place in her heart, and mine.

Animal and Human Behavior

Sometimes our pets need to communicate specific problems or concerns to their humans. When these are not addressed, we assume we have to modify their behavior with training. Generally, most people start with "sit," "stay," and "down" training. These are good beginnings and you should make sure that your new puppy knows what these verbal commands mean. But not all behaviors can be redirected by good training, as in the first story.

Brutos

Brutos, a four-year-old male Boston terrier, had been in the same household for all his life. His mother was also a family pet and he remained with them because he was the runt. Much later, the family adopted a boxer, another male named Spike, who recently got a girlfriend named Jasmine, another boxer. (We first met the family in chapter 7 when Spike got lost.)

In our session, the first image Brutos sent me of himself was as a huge Great Dane; he thought he was one, at least in personality and ego. This was a very funny image for me because in real life he stood barely eight inches from the ground. He really thought he was as big as his Great Dane neighbors, which was why he would bark up a storm, thinking he intimidated them. He felt comfortable parading around and telling others not to invade his property. Mom confirmed that they lived next door to two huge Great Danes and that Brutos would go out into the yard and bark at them through the fence.

Brutos's issue and the reason for my visit was that he'd been drinking excessive amounts of water lately and, of course, disposing of it as urine in and around the household. When I asked how much was an excessive amount, Ricky (the mom) said, "I stopped counting after he drank two gallons in one day. I took him to the vet, who ran the usual blood tests and found the results normal. He suggested Brutos's problem was not physical but psychological and that I should get in touch with you."

Brutos continued, "I am the alpha dog and therefore in charge of the household. My duties are many and I like it that way. But I need to mark my territory to keep reminding the other two that I'm in charge and that the house, inside and out, is my domain. Everything that needs to be done should go through me first, and done only with my permission. I need the water to keep my command."

Ricky, who was concerned for his health and well-being, asked him if he knew that so much water was bad for his heart. After some thought, he agreed to curb his consumption a little but still requested to have at least twice the amount of water he would normally require.

Ricky obliged, and the whole family worked together toward letting Brutos know he was the top dog of the family. He got fed first, walked first, petted first, and had the pick of the beds for the evening. Ricky subsequently called me to report that he was doing much better and, even more remarkably, was limiting his marking to only outside the house.

There is always a reason for a pet's odd behavior, but sometimes the behavior develops out of something that happened in the house that was, to the animal, somehow traumatic, as in the next case.

Freddy

Lois called me in to communicate with both her dogs. She had no specific concerns but wanted to know if there was anything she could do to make their life happier. One of them, Freddy, was half poodle and half Dandie Dinmont terrier (see photograph, page 106). As soon as we started to talk, Freddy began telling me that he felt very tired and didn't have enough stamina to go for long walks. Suddenly, a ringing telephone interrupted his thoughts and he immediately began to whine, then bark, and then cry again. He took a while to calm down to the point that I was able to resume our telepathic conversation and, when we did, he wanted to talk about the phone.

Freddy told me in images and feelings that every time the phone rang it was bad news. He remembered a long time ago when Lois had picked up the phone and became upset. She began crying and he didn't like to see that. It hurt him to watch his mom suffering so much and he told me that he would rather she didn't pick up the phone anymore.

I explained this to Lois and asked, "Can you remember what he's talking about?"

Lois replied, "Yes. When he was two, my mother called to tell me my aunt was diagnosed with cancer and didn't have long to live. I remember crying on the phone. I can't remember whether he started whining at that exact time, but it's very close."

"What I suggest, Lois, is to get a phone with a different ringer. Then recondition Freddy to think that every time the new phone rings, it's good news. So as soon as you hear the phone ring, shout something like, 'Good. That's wonderful!' Then give Freddy a cookie or treat just before picking up the receiver."

I sent Freddie an image of a change and cookies coming his way if he would realize that a ringing phone doesn't mean bad news at all but, on the contrary, a treat!

I'm happy to report that the new phone did the trick. Freddy stopped whining and is now nonchalant when he hears the phone ring. Of course, even years later, he still expects a cookie.

Freddy

Sunshine

One day I received a long-distance call from New Jersey. Alice wanted me to talk with Sunshine, a seven-month-old Pomeranian female. Sunshine was just a baby and had a lot of issues that Alice needed to understand and correct.

Alice explained, "Sunshine is left alone for most of the day, enclosed in the kitchen area with plenty of toys, water, food, and a doggy litter box. Because we live in an apartment, the litter box seems the perfect training tool for a little dog. Sunshine is making real progress at using it, but won't go until I'm watching or my mother comes over for a daytime visit."

Sunshine's problem was that she was stuck on praise. Yes, it seemed that she wanted to be praised so much that she thought she only had to go when someone was there! It was a little misunderstanding that didn't take long to correct, but the most interesting part of the consultation was yet to happen.

During our talk, Alice asked Sunshine whether she liked the music that she left playing on the boom box. Sunshine complained, "The last time, the music had a lot of noise and bangs in it, and I did not enjoy it at all."

Alice laughed. "I left a heavy metal CD playing by mistake yesterday. I meant to ask about the CD of nature sounds I bought specially for Sunshine."

Sunshine said, "Yes, and I would like to hear the radio sometimes too, but if Mom wants to play some music, then I'd rather listen to country."

Alice, a modern young woman, laughed. "Out of all the music Sunshine could possibly ask for, she has to pick the one I really dislike. There's no way!"

We quickly changed the subject, so imagine my surprise to receive the following e-mail a week later:

Dear Dr. Monica:

I wanted to write and thank you for your time and help with Sunshine. I can't thank you enough. Already, I am seeing a more considerate Sunshine. I also switched the CDs back to the softer music, but gave her a choice when we went to bed the other night.

I found a Shania Twain CD I like that is classified as country music, though I hate to admit it and usually don't. I offered her a choice between that and heavy metal. I showed them both to her and told her what each one was. I was so shocked when she began to paw at the Shania Twain CD. I couldn't believe my eyes!

I tried again, mixing them up behind my back and switching them around, then laying them on the floor, gesturing towards them and saying, "Country or heavy metal," not really specifying which was which. But she had already seen them and could tell the difference in the pictures. She quickly went to the Shania Twain CD, pawed at it again, sat back down and began to whine. Then she pawed at it some more and looked at me. I was so happy that she had done that and had actually connected with me and let me know she truly did prefer that one.

I put the CD in immediately and, as I went to brush my teeth, I noticed her in my bathroom mirror, standing on her hind legs and spinning around happily! Your consultation definitely made a difference and every time I play that CD, she gets up on her hind legs and spins around happily or wants to dance with me. I haven't taken it out of the boom box yet!

Thank you again for all your help!

Alice

Animal and Human Behavior

Sometimes all our pets need to know is how we feel about them and what our plans are. This was the case in the next story.

Angel

Angel, a female Rhodesian ridgeback (see photograph, page 110), had been adopted from a shelter and was extremely shy. She had been with her new family for a couple of months before I went to see them. Judy, her mom, explained, "Angel spends most of the day hiding out in a bedroom upstairs and only comes down to eat. No one can touch her without her immediately urinating on herself. Sometimes when she's called for dinner, she pees because the voice is too loud. And sometimes she just pees because someone walks rapidly by her."

Judy had to get a leash on Angel before she could convince her that it was okay to come downstairs and visit with me. While Judy went to the kitchen to get me a drink of water, I tried to communicate to Angel that everything was going to be all right and that she should talk with us so we could get to the bottom of any problems she might have. Angel sat down next to me and, after about five minutes, lay down on my feet and remained there the whole time we communicated.

Angel told me, "I was not told that this was my new family. I thought that it was a test to see how good I was and so, to be good, I spend as much time as I can in the bedroom, out of everybody's way."

Judy told her, "No matter what, you are part of this family for good. We love you very much and I promise you that you'll never go back to the shelter. We only wish you would be happy and enjoy life a little more. Try not to be so scared. No one will ever hit you. And don't worry about peeing all the time. We will clean it up. I think you're a beautiful girl and just like your namesake, a little Angel. There is absolutely nothing wrong with you and the whole family feels the same way. We love you."

When I opened my eyes, Angel was sitting up, her face close to mine. She put her head down on my lap and her right front paw on my knees. Judy was amazed. "Angel has never done that with anyone. Is this common for you?"

I told her, "Most of my clients have their own way of thanking me for their communication. Many do so by opening their heart and offering their love in the only way they know how."

Judy got her camera and took a picture of us (below) because, as she said, "Nobody will believe me otherwise."

Angel

Animal and Human Behavior

I saw Judy two months later and she told me, "Angel has had only one incident but she's been a new dog since your visit. Her confidence is much higher and she spends a lot less time in the bedroom. She even runs to the front door to greet people when guests come to the house."

Confidence is vitally important to some animals. The next case is a good example of this, this time from an e-mail client who saw my website (www.petcommunicator.com) and wrote to me.

Rosco

Jan had a little one-year-old dachshund named Rosco. She lived in a rural area and was afraid to leave Rosco out in the back yard with his big brother Dakota, a yellow Labrador. Her first dachshund had been taken by an eagle, wriggled free of its talons, but had broken his back on hitting the ground. His spinal cord had been severed and he'd needed to be euthanized. This bad experience remained with her and she refused to let this dog suffer the same fate. So Rosco spent his days pining alone inside the house, looking out the window at Dakota enjoying the outdoors.

Rosco had plenty of toys he could play with during the day. Jan gave him a chew before she left for work. He had his newspapers to go potty, as he'd been trained to do, and he had a large, comfortable dog bed. However, I learned all these important points after the fact.

Jan told me, "I wanted a consultation because Rosco has been relieving himself on the rug during the day instead of on his papers and I was wondering if everything is okay with him. One day he even chewed a big hole in the couch, and another day he chewed up an expensive rug."

As soon as we were in contact, Rosco complained, "Mom treats me like a little boy when, in fact, I'm all grown up. I long to be free and go out and play with Dakota. I'm mad that I am trapped in the house

Animal and Human Behavior

alone for so many hours. I'm tired of my toys and upset at everything. Even Dad belittles me because I can't prove I'm a real dog like Dakota, who goes hiking and hunting with him. I want some freedom, and I want it now!"

When I translated this for Jan, I suggested that they put in a doggy door to give Rosco access to the outside, but she politely refused, giving me all the reasons why she could not leave Rosco outside all day long, which I promptly translated to him. Next, I suggested some bargaining that sometimes works. "Why not put a chair by the back window with a pillow or cushion so that Rosco can enjoy a better view of the back yard, maybe watching the birds and the squirrels?"

Ignoring my suggestion, Jan insisted, "And remind him to start using his newspapers again," which I conveyed to him.

Lastly, we talked about his destructive behavior. When Rosco insisted again that he needed to have access to the back yard, Jan explained to him, "A new rule of 'time outs' will be imposed if you continue to be destructive inside the house. That means spending a few minutes in the bathtub while being ignored."

Jan was satisfied with the reading and promised to keep in touch. Her e-mail updates tell the story.

Thursday, August 10

I got home yesterday to find a disaster. Rosco had gotten the dirty laundry out and spread it around the house and chewed the rug again. Is it common for a dog to get like that after a communication? I gave him a time out, and when he cried, I told him, "Quiet, you're in time out."

This morning, I put a chair with a pillow in front of the window so he can see out and left the radio on. I also used the cleaner on the carpet and drops on his paper. I will let you know how it goes.

Animal and Human Behavior

Friday, August 11

I wish I could say things were better but this time it was about 300 percent worse, the worst he has EVER been. I had a bag full of packing peanuts and he got that and his dog food and scattered them together from one end of the house to the other. I had put a pillow on a chair by the window so he could see out, and he chewed that. He chewed a hole in the couch and holes in the entryway rug. I put him in time out in the tub in the bathroom for fifteen minutes. Rosco KNEW he had been very bad and was pretty much down in the dumps all evening. Tonight we are going shopping for a doggy door. In the meantime, Rosco is confined to a ten-by-ten area in the basement with the lights on. He has a blanket (not his favorite), a small rug that he will probably shred, water, his papers, a toy, and a couple of chewies. I am sure that I feel worse about leaving him there than he feels about being there. Oh, on the bright side, during his day yesterday, he used his papers instead of the carpet.

Monday, August 14

This morning when I left for work, I left the doggie door open. Jon installed the door Friday night and Rosco can now go in and out all day, play with his brother Dakota, and chase the cats and birds. I leave the door open except for at night. Rosco is using the door regularly and staying outside more than normal.

Yesterday, Jon and I left Rosco and Dakota and went for a motorcycle ride for about an hour. When we came home, everything was fine. I am hoping that having Dakota there will help him feel more secure and less destructive.

Monday, August 14

Good news!! Rosco must have spent most of his day out-doors. Jon just called me to say that when he got home, Rosco came in the house for about two minutes and then headed back out to hang out in the yard. I am hoping and praying that this doggy door is the answer. Tomorrow I am taking him to the vet to get microchipped.

Well, it is time for me to go home, I just wanted to let you know the good news!

Wednesday, August 16

There is a happy voice behind this e-mail. I guess Rosco just wanted to be a big boy and go outside. Ever since he got his door, he has been VERY good. We have not had any reason to have a time out. He is getting more independent as well. This is good, although he is not as interested in coming when called the first time. I can work on that.

Thank you so much for your help. I will let you know if the trouble returns, although I don't think it will.

I told Jan that I was very proud of her. Getting in touch with your animal and allowing communication is only half the trip. You still need to apply what you learn and follow up. Their requests are seldom im-material. They ask for something when they really mean it. You need to be willing to change with them. It is impossible for me to ask them to do something just because you wish it; there must be give-and-take. They always give us unconditional love; surely we can give some too. A pet door is very important to an animal's sense of independence, as we also see in the next case.

Reber

Beth called me crying one day and left a tearful message on my answering machine. Reber, her dog, was an escape artist, and Beth was at her wit's end. Reber had twice climbed up the neighbor's wall and had chewed her way out of the back yard on several occasions.

Reber was not really a "dog" in the common sense but a basenji, a mixture of a dog that does not bark and a cat that grooms and has a mind of her own. She climbed trees quite well but didn't get the hang of coming down. Fences were no problem either. Reber was less than six months old when I met her.

I arrived early one morning and Reber met me at the door with a warbling sound. Since they don't bark, they make a gurgling sound in their throats as a greeting. She did this three times and Beth couldn't get over this surprising display of emotion.

When I closed my eyes, Reber's personality came through right away. She was hyper, with a high-pitched voice and a rapid succession of statements and questions for Beth, who had asked all of us to stay in the kitchen area. "Why did you close the door? Why are you closing all the doors to the house? That's not right, you never do that! Am I supposed to be here? I don't think it's right. I need some room!"

I told Beth that Reber would soon calm down and, after a while, she was articulate and well able to explain her feelings. She boasted proudly, "I go to work every day."

Dad agreed while Mom laughed, "Every morning I ask Reber, 'Are you ready to go to work?'"

Reber continued, "I take my job very seriously. I'm needed here."

"In fact," Mom said, "Reber is a good hunter. She took care of a couple of mice just last week. What I want to know is how we can convince her not to jump the fence."

Reber came right back with the answer for them. "Do not leave me outside where I can't see what's happening. Allow me to come and go

Reber

with a door and I will feel a lot more comfortable. And I worry when you are gone, so tell me when you are coming back!"

That was easy. All they had to do was install a doggy door and give Reber some freedom.

Reber was so thankful to be able to express her feelings that she began circling the dinette table where the three of us sat. Then she came around my left side and put one paw on my lap, then a second. Since I didn't tell her to stop, she lifted up a third leg and finally

Animal and Human Behavior

squeezed the fourth one up. Her movements were very catlike and delicate. She placed her head in the crook of my right elbow and was fast asleep within minutes. We'd had a great communication and talked about many things. Beth took a photo of us (see page 116) and sent it to me with a note: "Reber has never tried to leave our yard again. Thank you."

Crista

Angella left a distraught message on my machine: "Dr. Monica, you have to come see Crista again. There is something wrong. She's doing something she's never, ever done before. She actually peed on my bed! You have to help us! Call me ASAP!"

I'd seen Angella and Crista six months earlier. Crista, a nine-year-old female cat, was a domestic shorthair with white fur and gray spots. She was a very determined lady. I had met them earlier, when Angella's other cat, Molly, had to be put down for medical reasons. Crista had wanted another companion but, this time, insisted on being involved in the choosing process. She reminded us that she was the queen of the house and that she only wanted someone who would readily submit to her whims. Crista got her wish and a new addition to the household was adopted from the Humane Society.

On the way to the session with them, I wondered if something was wrong between Crista and the new cat. Again, like so many other times, I was to be proven wrong.

As soon as I arrived, Crista came to see me and let out a very loud meow, which was unusual behavior for her since she does not like people that much.

I sat on the couch and she couldn't wait to start talking. "Mom is coming home with a different smell lately. She goes out for a few hours, and then smells like dog. How can I tell her that I disapprove of that? I know what she's up to, though. She has a new boyfriend!"

When I relayed this to Angella, she was stunned. She told Crista, "I thought you liked Travis. He comes in to visit with you and is very nice."

Crista replied haughtily, "He only tries to be nice to me because he knows how much you love me, but he is not a cat person. Does he own a dog?"

Angella replied, "Yes, but how do you know?"

"I can smell it on you. I can smell the dog in your hair."

Angella tried to reason with Crista. "That is no reason for you to pee on the bed. After all, you sleep there every night, too. But now that I know it bothers you, I'll be more careful about not bringing other pet's smells into the house."

Crista took this conversation in stride but agreed with Angella that she would not express her feelings by peeing on the bed. Angella, in turn, agreed to change clothes as soon as she got home, as well as wash her hands and face before going to bed.

Crista and her mom happily worked out a give-and-take arrangement. The next story, also about peeing, is quite amusing as well.

Francis and William

Mary called me in to see her two cats because, after years of living together, one of them had started peeing on the bed. William was a beautiful orange tabby male, about five years old. Francis was another male, black and white.

After a tour of the house, we ended up at the crime scene—the bedroom. I saw nothing unusual there and it was obvious that both cats, who had followed us upstairs, were very comfortable in that room. I sat on the floor while Mary and her husband sat on the bed. William came to me, smelled me, then lay down beside me. He did not beat around the bush and came to the point right away. "This is my room. I sleep here and come here when I want to be alone. I do not appreciate it when they (meaning Mom and Dad) change things. I have been smelling something very annoying at the foot of the bed lately and I can't tell where the smell is coming from."

I looked around again and everything seemed fine. The bed was made, they had a beautiful afghan at the foot of the bed, and Mary pointed to the spot where William lies down to sleep. I asked, "Have you bought any bedding that could account for the new smell that William is complaining about?"

She said no.

"Have you changed detergents or any other cleaning solution?"

Again, the answer was no.

So I went back to William and asked him more questions. "Where is the smell coming from? What kind of smell? Where are you when this happens?"

William could only tell me, "I'm already in bed by the time I smell it, and it comes from the inside of the bed, but only the bottom half."

I asked Dad, "Are you wearing any creams from the waist down?"

Imagine my surprise when he said, "Yes! I've been putting some medication on at night!"

"Well, there you have it," I exclaimed triumphantly. "William is complaining about this new smell. He doesn't even know it's still you. I want you to take William to the bathroom with you tonight and let him smell the cream, then put the cream on as always and let him smell you again."

Dad was laughing so hard he was in tears. "I can't believe I have to let my cat smell my medicine."

I told William what the plan was and left confident that we'd gotten to the bottom of that problem!

Six months later, Mary called me for another communication. They were going on vacation and she wanted the boys to know about it. "Oh, and by the way," she added, "after William smelled the medicine, he never had another incident again."

Animal and Human Behavior

Believe it or not, our animals can smell things we can't. They are sensitive to any smell and any changes. Think of that next time you change your perfume or cologne.

CHAPTER 9

Our Feathered Friends

I have always had a thing for feathers. I love to touch them, feel how soft they are, study how they fit together, and enjoy their intricate patterns, especially their colors. I have a flower vase on my desk holding a collection of beautiful feathers. I look at them every day and delight in their form, but have never had a pet bird. In fact, I know next to nothing about them, and there is a lot to learn.

Humans who share their life with birds must know exactly what to feed them and what to keep away from them, the temperature they feel comfortable living with (depending on where they are originally from), and as much information as possible to prevent them from getting sick and dying suddenly, without explanation. (Birds are renowned for masking symptoms of illness right up to the point of death.)

It goes almost without saying that you need to put in time and effort to teach them to talk. Some scientists say bird talk is simple repetition of what they hear and that it's impossible for a brain the size of a pea to process thoughts. Many bird owners disagree.

As always, I approach my clients with respect and with a clear mind. Without prejudgment, I enter into a two-way conversation with their birds and just open myself up to the images they send me. Using this technique, I have learned that our feathered friends have real concerns and will, in their own way, communicate their wants and dislikes, as can any four-legged friend.

I am happy when I am called to a household with many animals in it, especially when there are different species, for there is a special kind of interaction among them that at times makes me laugh. This is one of them.

Spud

Two weeks prior to my visit, Mark and Donna had merged two households together. Donna had brought two cats with her; Mark, one cat and a double yellow-headed parrot named Spud.

They were delighted to move in together and start a new life, but their animal friends were not so sure this was such a good idea. The whole family was in distress. After two weeks of fights, they called me to help break the ice.

Spud

The parrot who loved when his daddy whistled.

Mark and Donna had made a very serious mistake. They had put the household together from day one without giving the animals time to get used to each other's scent and proximity. Fortunately, they'd moved into a new place, so this was neutral territory for all the animals, but each of them had needed time to adjust . . . and didn't get it. They were all trying to find their place and, in the process, fighting. Also, they needed to establish a hierarchy among themselves, and that was the most difficult thing of all. (Compare this with the more measured approach in "The Perfect Love Story" in chapter 10.)

Donna's older cat, Lulu, had been very sick after the move and was taken to the vet. She'd lost a lot of weight and had scabs all over her body. Donna was very concerned about Lulu, who had always been a follower, not a leader, and very shy and introverted. Lulu was obviously suffering from stress and anxiety over the move and the new arrivals. She had stopped eating, was restless around the house, and lately had taken to hiding inside the closet for privacy. She was afraid of Mark's cat, Smokey, who would jump out and scare her.

Once we began talking, Lulu requested some privacy. "A place where I can feel safe without any intruders. A place where I can nap and know I won't be jumped on, scratched at, or in any way scared. I'm tired of sleeping with one eye always open. I just need to rest."

The animals gave their suggestions about rearranging feeding schedules and food bowls to meet with everyone's desires and about adding more litter boxes so that the cats wouldn't have to share the most basic of needs. Mom and Dad were also told how to allocate time for each animal play and interaction with them.

Smokey was a grand old lady and quick to point out that she was the matriarch and therefore in charge of the household. She told me, "It's my responsibility to tell everyone their place and to keep order in the house. If someone is unruly, I let them know by whatever means I can. It's up to me to be top cat since my breed is the oldest and wisest of them all." (Smokey was part Siamese and part Burmese, and she was referring to her Siamese half.)

She went on, "I need to correct the other cats on etiquette and feel that it will take a long time for the others to understand it. Spud, on the other hand, makes me laugh. We are friends and I love that little bird!"

Mark agreed. "Smokey used to lie under Spud's cage in the other house to keep her company and I know very well that Smokey loves Spud. In this new house, however, Spud has a room all to herself. She has a beautiful iron cage with lots of food, toys, mirrors, and a delightful perch next to the window, but she's alone all day. Smokey doesn't even go into the room."

Our Feathered Friends

When I connected with Spud, I was surprised at her attitude toward Mark. "I am very upset with him. He no longer talks to me and spends no time with me. Even though I have a room all to myself, what I really want is to spend time with him, as we used to. I miss him too much."

Underscoring her thoughts with a piercing scream, she exclaimed, "Look at me! Look at my feathers! I am dirty and in distress! I also need something to peck at, something that I can eat that won't upset my stomach. And I need to keep busy! The thing I miss the most is Mark whistling to me. I used to love that. Make Mark promise that he will do it soon."

Mark was visibly shaken by this news and said, "With everything that's been going on in the house, I've had no time to share with Spud. I know how much she loves to play the whistle game, so tell her that I promise to begin right away."

Donna was trying very hard to make friends with Spud, but Spud was Daddy's little girl and jealous of the attention Mark was paying to Donna. Nevertheless, Spud promised she would give Donna time and allow some petting occasionally.

Mark and Donna were relieved that I'd been able to translate their animals' concerns and promised to keep me posted on progress. A few days later I received this note:

> Wow! Thanks, we have had some pretty exciting changes in our Animal Kingdom since your visit. Lulu has been getting much better, her skin almost completely healed. Only a small patch under her chin has not healed. She is eating better, too. Lulu and Smokey have had no more confrontations. They are both much calmer and pass by each other and sleep within a few feet without needing to exchange hostile words.
>
> Smokey seems calmer, too, and not so cranky with us or the other cats. I am off to get her a separate litter box now, since she has not been using the cat door and persists in leaving

land mines in the back bedroom. She has never used a litter box before, so I will leave the directions out for her.

I can't thank you enough for the changes in Spud's attitude since you two spoke. The next day she was much more open to interaction and came to me within seconds of approaching her cage to play. I took her outside for a bath and a walk around the block to dry off. All day non-stop jabbering, and yes, we played the "whistle game" for hours, too. The following day I brought her out and we watched a couple of movies together on the couch and then she made her move. She began preening my ear, neck, and hair. This might seem kinky to some, but she liked it. Later, when I returned her to her cage, she wanted more attention and refused to go in, so I gave her a quick kiss on the beak and took her back to the couch. That was enough foreplay for her and she went for it. She started kissing my lips and then, while I was laughing, stuck her whole head in my mouth for a full dental inspection. She has not been this affectionate in years. Thank you!

We believe that your visit has made a significant impact on our animals' behavior.

Multi-species households are always great fun as they all try to get along together. But sometimes achieving that harmony can take time and thought. How, for example, do you introduce a new animal into a household that already has pets? I usually give the following advice to my clients.

Before you bring the animal in the house, picture it in your mind as vividly and as detailed as possible, from nose to tail. Include as many features as you can, especially its name, if you know it. Say the name out loud, too. This will help the existing animals to understand that the name belongs to the prospective resident.

Take time to introduce the animals. For cats, keep them separate for a week, allowing them to smell the new arrival through a closed door. Then exchange their beds so that they can get used to the other's scent. Another day, exchange rooms for a period of fifteen minutes. On the next day, leave the door open a crack so they can see each other. If they wish, they are free to push the door open and meet under supervision. Then, finally, give them the run of the house.

Dogs are easier and we can immediately introduce them under a watchful eye. Do not leave them alone until you are sure that they are fine with each other.

When the animals finally meet each other, they will take care of their own introductions. Always treat your established animals with respect, by greeting, feeding, and petting them first, then giving attention to the new arrival.

Over time, carefully watch the animals' behavior: who grooms whom, who defers to whom, who gets the pick of the favorite places. As the human, you need to make sure that you follow the pecking order. Eventually, one animal will become top dog or cat—even though it may be a newer addition.

If bringing two families together can cause problems, a family splitting up through divorce can cause tremendous upheavals in their pets' lives. I have done a couple of consultations that involved the divorce of Mom and Dad. In one case, they had three animals; in the other, two. Since the parents could not choose, they allowed the animals to do it for them.

The first thing the animals need to know, as with children, is that they are loved and did nothing wrong. It's not their fault that Mom and Dad are splitting up. To accomplish this, both people should send feelings of love, hugs, and thanks to their pets. Do this in your mind's eye. Then imagine a picture of Mom and Dad together that gets torn down the middle from top to bottom, so that the two slowly separate in the picture. At this point, if one of the animals physically goes to one of the partners, include that animal's picture on either Mom's side or Dad's side, emphasizing who is going with whom. Say the animal's names in your mind. After each step, remind them they are loved and that they are not at fault. Run a movie in your head that shows the animals eating, sleeping, walking, and playing alone from now on. If you're not sure whether you're succeeding, just pretend that you are; when beginning animal communication, many people really are succeeding but don't realize it immediately.

The next story is also about a home with several different animal species.

The Lovebirds

When I arrived at Karen's home, she had separated her animals in every room of the house and took me for a tour to meet all of them. I met a huge, colorful parrot; a cockatoo; cats; rabbits; and tropical fish. After holding a brief session for each, that left just a pair of lovebirds, and Karen was concerned about them. "They get stressed every time I clean their cage. It's hard to catch them as they fly desperately from one end of the cage to the other and they get upset at my attempts to hold them. Also, they don't like to be petted. I want them to know that it's a good feeling when done with all my love."

I made contact and sent them images about staying calm during the cleaning and promised them that Mom would put their toys back in the same places. They in turn requested a perch to stand on while the cage was being cleaned.

Then I attempted to send them pictures of how humans need to touch to express their feelings of love and that, when done with care, it is a soothing feeling. They received this information with a little skepticism but promised to try it.

Just when I thought the session was over, I told Karen, "One of them has a question for you, but I can't tell which bird it is. I keep getting two superimposed images, as if I have two x-rays in my mind's eye, and they keep superimposing and switching back and forth. This is the first time it's ever happened to me and I can't figure it out. Anyway, their question to you is, 'Mom, why can't we have any babies?'"

Because I receive images through my third eye, I close my eyes during a consultation, so I couldn't see the reaction of Karen or her husband to this question. Because the silence lasted longer than I expected, I thought she hadn't heard me so I asked again. "Why can't we have any babies?"

After another long silence, Karen said, "We think they're both females because they lay a lot of eggs but they never get fertilized!"

In my wildest dreams, I would not have imagined that! A lot of things were unclear to me at that point. First, how could I have known from their images being superimposed that I was actually seeing two female birds? Second, and for the skeptic inside of me, how could I have come up with that particular question? I had no idea they were laying a lot of eggs. Apparently, both of them were laying and sitting on the nest. Because both were laying, the nesting box had more than its normal share. The birds took turns sitting on the nest.

Third, why would I come up with a question of not being able to have babies? Karen never mentioned any of the above to me during my tour of the house. In fact, she hadn't even mentioned the lovebirds until right at the end of my visit. And I don't even remember if she told me their names!

Lastly, how is it possible for them to know so much that they want this specific question answered by the human who takes care of them?

It is revelations such as this that prompt me to continue with my line of work. To be able to give animals a voice and let them speak in their own words is the best feeling I could ever hope to have. Even if I wanted to be my worst enemy, my strictest skeptic, instances such as this convince me that what I am translating is for real and does not come from me. Clearly, it comes from genuine telepathic communication in the form of the images that I try to translate.

Outdoor cats often go missing and dogs run off and lose their sense of direction, and I have been involved in a lot of those cases. But how exactly do you lose a bird that is confined to his cage in the living room and not allowed to fly outside? This was the big mystery that I hoped to solve in the next story, never thinking that an animal's words would lead to criminal proceedings.

Alex

At the home, I was greeted by a husband and wife, two daughters, one teenage son, and a baby. A black Labrador female named Ashley and four cats rounded out the family.

It's rare to have the whole family involved in the process and even more rare to have a male teenager listening as well. I recorded the session for future reference.

We sat down in the living room and surveyed all that remained of Alex, the missing African grey: his cage—a huge wrought-iron black beauty that occupied a good deal of space—with its door still open, and a few tiny feathers scattered on the floor and inside the cage. Next to it was a perch on which Alex had spent most of his days. The food bowls were full and untouched.

Mom told me, "We came home from work that night and found he wasn't here. We searched inside and out, and found no more than two feathers in the front yard, but they were so tiny that we were not sure they could be his. Alex just disappeared without a trace."

With four cats in residence, my first thought was that one of them might have had an extra serving of lunch, even though an African grey would put up quite a fight. When I voiced my concerns, Dad explained, "When I first got Alex, I spent several nights sleeping in the living room with the cats to teach them that the bird was now part of the family and that they needed to accept him. Every time a cat would be interested in the bird, I was right there, ready to intervene if necessary. Even Ashley respected the bird, who would keep her company and call her by name to be next to him, as most talking birds do."

I started the consultation by first talking to all the animals in residence and asking if anyone had seen or heard anything that would give the family a clue. Two of the cats told me that on the day Alex disappeared, they'd already gone outside for their daytime outings. Another cat said that she'd been sleeping in another room and heard someone talking. The fourth told me, "I was hiding under the Christmas tree and saw a young man squeeze through the dog door and into the living room. I didn't see exactly what happened, and then he left. I know that the gardener had already left for the day and this happened shortly afterwards. But it was still morning and the whole family was gone."

The family had lots of questions but the cats couldn't answer them, so I decided to get in touch with Alex himself to see if he could answer some questions. He came in crystal clear and right away. He said, "I was forcefully taken from the house by a kid. I fought all the way out the door, and almost made it free."

He went on to describe how he was put in a vehicle, and complained about being roughly handled and how, all of a sudden, everything went dark and silent. "Right now, I am inside a box. There were three of them, and Matt [the family's teenage son] knows them. One of them has a lot of hair parted in the middle with big loops on either side. The second has a nose like me, big and pointed. When he looks at me, that's the only thing I clearly see. The third has a really round face. All of them wear a lot of black or very dark clothing."

The family plied me with many more questions, including names, location, type of car, etc. Alex became impatient and said, "Let me describe the room I am in. It's a mess. I'm standing in a corner and behind me is a small window. When I look out, I can see that I'm on the second floor of a house. The kid who lives in that room is always on the computer. There's a light with a blue or purple tint under a desk or counter. I have never seen one like that in our home. It's very unusual."

When prompted about whether he was eating at all, he said, "I was offered pizza and some green stuff that I didn't recognize and would not eat. I'm kept in a box where it is dark."

I relayed to him, "At night the family goes looking for you and calls out your name. Have you ever heard anyone calling you?"

"No, I don't hear anyone."

That was as much as I could get for them but the whole family was encouraged by this and, spurred on by knowing that their beloved parrot was still alive, they set the wheels in motion to try to find him.

Upset by Alex telling him that he knew these kids, Matt immediately put two and two together and recognized them from his description. They were two brothers and a friend. He wanted to leave and confront them right then and there, but Dad interceded.

Mom later called me. "Dad and Matt went over to the brothers' home to see if Alex was in the house. The brothers were home alone without adult supervision. Dad went in to check out the older boy's room, who was Matt's friend, and found absolutely nothing. They went to the young brother's room and froze in their tracks. The room was a mess. A window looked down on the side yard from the second floor. The computer was there and, just above it, a purple light shone down on the desk." (Dad later told me, "It was so exactly as you described it that I almost peed in my pants!")

Unfortunately, several days had passed since my talk with Alex and he was no longer there. The kids denied all knowledge and the search came to an abrupt stop. The family could not rest, however, and hired a private investigator to follow the kids around, who finally broke down. They confessed to taking Alex from the house, keeping him for a couple of days, and selling him to a pet store, telling the owner that

Our Feathered Friends

they no longer wanted the bird. The pet store had sold the bird to a woman for a Christmas present. The police were called in and Alex was happily reunited with his family almost three weeks after the kidnapping.

Nowadays, Alex enjoys not only his freedom but also a family that would not give up on him and thinks he is the smartest bird in the whole wide world. I agree!

Sometimes birds become separated from their people by accident, as in the next case.

The Baby Parrot

Sandra called me because she had found a baby parrot and wanted to know if I could pick up where he came from. The little parrot related his story to me and I relayed it to Sandra over the phone. "My mom is a girl with blonde hair. I was loose in her bedroom and decided to try out my wings. I didn't know I could fly so high. Suddenly I was tired and scared. I landed on the roof, but realized that they all looked exactly the same and I didn't know which one was mine.

"I heard voices and made my way down from the roof very carefully. Then I saw someone who looks like Mom, only bigger, so I felt at home and promised myself never to leave again. I need to keep a close eye on my new mom to make sure she is always around."

He explained to me how he enjoys a soft human finger run gently up through his chest and on top of his head. Then he showed me another picture of how his head bobs up and down in delight.

"I have a cage where I am at night, and sometimes during the day, but when the girl is at home, I am loose in her bedroom. When the cat is inside the house, I get scared. I do not like cats. I like it here with this new mom because there are no cats and I'm happy to hear the sound of kids' voices."

Sandra told me, "My daughter has blonde hair. The parrot follows her around the house from room to room, not letting her out of his sight. Even though the window is open, he stays away from it. The most important clue you gave me is that we live in a condo complex where all the houses have the same color and type of roof!"

I don't know whether Sandra ever found the bird's previous mom but, either way, it has a good home. Sadly, as we saw in chapter 7, so few lost animal cases have happy endings. Most animals realize that they are lost when they find themselves in unusual surroundings or when their senses are telling them that their "radar" to go back home is no longer working. They will always try to find a common thing—a smell, a sight, or a similar person. Many times it is just their gut feeling that they will be welcomed into a particular home.

Remember: when you open your arms and your hearts to a lost pet, you are in fact accepting an invitation to share your lives. Don't take it for granted!

CHAPTER 10

Rabbits and a Love Story

I didn't know the first thing about rabbits when I was called in for a rabbit consultation. Coming from another country—and a big city at that—I could not conceive of anyone having a rabbit for a pet, but this is America, I reminded myself, and anything is possible. So off I went.

Tabby and Fiona

In the previous chapter, we met Karen and her husband, Andy, who lived in a large apartment. When she called, she had recently lost a cat, but also wanted a follow-up reading for all her other pets as well—four rabbits, a cockatoo, a parrot, two lovebirds, fish, and two cats!

On arriving at her place, I noticed that the rabbits were not contained in a cage but had full run of the dining room area. Boxes for hiding, tubing for playing, and several cat toys were scattered on the floor. Their serving dish was full of freshly cut food, vegetables and leaves of all colors. They seemed happy and did not hide when they saw me.

In the corner of the room, a big parrot and an old cockatoo looked down from their perches, their cage behind them with the door open. The parrot was making *very* loud squawks.

A white cat appeared to say hello and inspect my smell and, from the back of the house, another cat sauntered in to meet me. Karen said, "This is a new arrival from the Irvine Animal Shelter. I named him Buddy."

Ethyl, the matriarch of the house and their first pet, was an old white cat. She told me, "I love to cuddle with Andy, who sits on the sofa to watch TV at night. If you had asked me two weeks ago whether I wanted another pet in the house, I would have said no, but today I feel good about having another cat, although much work remains to be done. I've tried to teach Buddy many things around the house, especially how to behave around so many other species. I am trying, but Buddy is too young and sometimes he does not pay attention. It will take time to train him just right."

When I talked to Buddy, he told me, "I'm glad to get away from the shelter, but sometimes it's very difficult for me to get used to the different sounds and smells of the house. Also, I don't understand why some of them don't want to play my games. I have to try very hard to entice them to play. The birds scare me, though, because they are too loud."

Rabbits and a Love Story

It was time to talk to the rabbits. Tabby, a calico Holland lop-eared male, was the oldest and the first in the family. He was very wise and told Karen, "You're always volunteering your time to do good, and should follow your dream of opening a sanctuary for animals. I assure you that you would be very good at it. You have a special connection with all animal species and should not let it go to waste."

Tabby was an old soul and had been around many times. What was most impressive was that he talked as if he were human. Initially, I had a hard time taking a rabbit seriously, but he made so much sense that I tried not to think about it and just focused on being an open channel for the information. He also had a special relationship with Ethyl, the white cat.

Tabby had no complaints; he liked his food and his girlfriend, and knew he was loved.

Later, Karen told me, "It's always been my dream to set up some kind of place for unwanted animals but, financially, I can't do it right now, so I volunteer at the local shelter, going daily to feed and care for unwanted rabbits."

Then we moved on to Tabby's girlfriend, Fiona, a beautiful soft brown female. Fiona was shy and frequently ran to hide inside the big cylinders around the edge of the dining area. Fiona complained, "I'm very hot in the summer and want the windows open, but I appreciate the ice water bottle that Mom provides for me in the mornings."

Mom said, "I'm concerned about Fiona's shyness. I would like her to feel secure at home and know that nothing will hurt her and that it's okay to be loved."

Fiona listened thoughtfully and then started to talk. "I am not happy about the new addition to the house," she said, and showed me an image of Buddy.

Karen said, "Yes, I'm concerned because Buddy wants to play with her and jumps out at her from every angle. Fiona gets scared and runs away. But Buddy, thinking this is a great game, follows her and,

Rabbits and a Love Story

in trying to catch her, he gets excited and uses his claws on her. Will you tell Fiona that she should not run, but retaliate if necessary to teach Buddy some boundaries? Because she hides in the cylinders, it's easy for him to get to her. Tell her to turn around and make it clear to Buddy that she is not interested in playing."

Fiona replied, "My heart starts pounding at the sight of Buddy, but I'll give it a try."

A few days later I received this e-mail:

Dear Dr. Monica,

Fiona (the brown lop in the living room, the "hot" one) let a rabbit person, a total stranger, pet her and even rub her cheeks! Oh, and the same night you were there, she and Tab sat in the middle of the living room floor and Buddy charged them from out on the deck. Tab moved away but Fiona stayed still. Buddy had to leap over her in total surprise when she didn't budge. She nudged his butt as soon as he hit the ground and she chased him! His days of chasing her are over. Thank you, thank you!

I have been in touch with Karen and involved with her pets for over two years. Later, she e-mailed me again:

Would you talk to Tabby and Fiona? They've started peeing and pooping around the living room, and we had to pen them up in the dining room, with a fence keeping them from going into the living room. They have their big litter box with hay and the tunnel under the dining table.

I want to know why they're peeing and pooping outside their litter box? If they are mad because I smell of other rabbits, that was not our deal. When you talked to them before, we agreed that, as long as I didn't bring any rabbits home with me, it was okay with Tab for me to go to the shelter. If that is the problem—that I smell of other rabbits—would you remind them of our deal? I love them very much, and I am allowed to spend time with other rabbits as long as I don't bring them home.

Do they know why they are fenced in now? Andy is really tired of the mess and we both want them to go back to their good litter box habits. Are they remembering how to use the litter box all the time by being kept inside the pen? I hate to have them confined to a small place, and I cannot wait until we can trust them again!

Thanks very much, Monica. You are a lifesaver!

My reply went like this:

Dear Karen:

I am pretty confident that Tabby is talking about Ethyl. The reason for this is that he keeps going back to asking who will be in charge of things. Ethyl!

Ethyl is the glue that keeps us all together, he says. She has been doing it for so long that he doesn't even remember a time when a problem could get resolved without her intervention.

Fiona, of course, wanted to volunteer, but Tabby insists this is not her turf. And he does not want to be in charge either. From there stems a lot of anxiety.

On the other hand, Ethyl knows that her time to go is near and she's okay with it. She appreciated your understanding and support. She too has been happy and was able to enjoy herself these past four years with you. But she is old and tired and needs to continue to evolve. She is slowly talking to everybody about her transition. Tabby, who is the smartest one, somehow does not want to hear her out. He is very attached. But Ethyl is set in her ways and will not leave until it is settled. She would prefer to go peacefully because she is not at this moment in a lot of pain, but if things change, she will let you know and hopes you will act on the information. Ethyl is positive that you two have a high degree of communication and it is not difficult for you to pick up on a pleading thought.

I mentioned to both Tabby and Fiona that they will have to remain in confinement until you get back from vacation and they both accept this information. They also asked me if Eric's mom [a neighboring rabbit's mom] is the one who will come in to give them food and I didn't know what to answer. I told them that whoever it is will follow your wishes and the same kind and amount of food will be served in your absence. They are okay with that. Fiona wants the window open when the air is not running, but I don't know if you are going to be able to do that while away, so I didn't give her an answer. All I told her was that I would relay the message.

Again, they are happy that they can "talk." I think they will be good with their habits upon your return, but take it easy anyway!

Hope this helps, Karen.

The next day I received this answer:

Thank you so very much, Monica.

I will spend more time with both Tab and Miss Ethyl, maybe both together, and see if I can get them to talk about things. He is very wise and will understand her if he will listen. He has always been kind of goofy about her since he first came to our house and fell in love with her, so maybe that is why it is hard for him. I will try to reassure him that we will all be okay; she will still be in our hearts.

He has been doing a lot of "gluing" himself, perhaps he doesn't realize it. He was the one who took Buddy in when he was new, and showed him what we expected of him, and taught him about the fun stuff.

During our vacation, we will have Velma, our pet sitter who came before, come in the mornings to feed everyone, turn on the A/C, and give Fiona a frozen water bottle. Laurie (Eric's mom) will come at night to feed and turn off the A/C and open the windows. So you did perfect with what you told them! Thank you.

I appreciate so very much what you do for us. I can relax now on vacation instead of wondering what is going on with the kids!

Love, Karen

Last minute update:

We couldn't convince Tabby to stay around and be in charge of the household. He made his transition on October 14, with Ethyl following him on October 17.

Mom celebrated their lives with a memorial, and a special card was sent out to friends with this poem, adapted from Edgar Guest's poem "To All Parents."

For Tabby: Companion, Teacher, and Friend

"I'll lend you, for a little while, a bunny of mine," He said.
"For you to love while he lives and mourn when he's dead.
It may be twelve or thirteen years or maybe less than three.
But will you, till I call him back, take care of him for me?

"He'll bring his charms to gladden you, and shall his stay be brief,
You'll have his lovely memories as solace for your grief.
I cannot promise he will stay, as all from earth return,
But there are lessons taught down there I want this bunny to learn.

"I've looked the whole world over in my search for teachers true,
And from the throngs that crowd life's lanes, I have selected you.
Now will you give him all your love—not think this labor vain,
Nor hate me when I come to call to take him back again."

I fancied that I heard them say, "Dear Lord, thy will be done."
For all the joy this bunn shall bring, the risk of grief we'll run.
We'll shower him with tenderness and love while we may,
And for the happiness we've known, forever grateful stay.

And should the angels call for him much sooner than we planned,
We'll brave the bitter grief that comes and try to understand.

Karen and Andy took great pains to prepare for their vacation away from their animals. You can do a lot to prepare your animals, to minimize their trauma. First, show your animals an image of where you are going. Show them that the house will be empty. Show them who will be coming in to feed and exercise them. In your mind (remember, animals communicate in pictures), look at a window that the animals usually look out of and show them how many days you are going to be gone by allowing days to turn into nights. Or, better yet, look at their food bowls and count how many times they will eat until you see each other again.

Finally, tell them that you are going on vacation and that you want them to be on vacation, too. Tell them they need to take it easy, that they do not have to guard the house or worry, and that they work so hard for you that you want them to enjoy themselves and have fun. (This is especially important if you're putting them into a boarding kennel.) And the really important part: *show them that you are coming back to get them!* Show them images of you actually coming in through the door, calling out their names, hugging them, cuddling them, embracing them—whatever you usually do. If possible, each member of the family should do this with each animal.

Subsequently, I've had several more consultations with rabbits and their people. Therefore I was a little more comfortable when I got my next call for a rabbit consultation. I didn't know this at the time, but this rabbit would forever change the way I look at them. Her story is a love story. I got her permission to tell it to you as well as the thumbs-up from her humans.

The Perfect Love Story

Millie and Rick have a white female rabbit, although they never use the "R word," preferring to say that they share their home with a princess who happens to be a rabbit. Her name is MisseySue.

Millie had called me for a consultation; about 90 percent of the time, it is women who are interested in such an "off the wall" topic but, when I got there, Millie asked me to wait for Rick, who was on his way home from work.

I saw the rabbit in the kitchen area. She had a large cage that was wide open, a very clean litter box, a large bowl of water, a food dish, and some hay. She had complete run of the kitchen area but a child's gate separated her from the living room area. Soon after we started talking, Millie removed the gate and gave the rabbit the run of the house. I must have looked at her strangely, for she assured me that MisseySue wouldn't soil any other place except in her litter box.

In front of the fireplace were some cardboard tunnels that Missey-Sue would run through and sometimes hide in, and some plastic toys were scattered around.

When Rick got home, he went to say hello first to MisseySue, and then to Millie. That told me who was first on his list! Before I started the session, I took time to thank him for being open and receptive to what I do. I told them about me, explained how I do it, and told them to ask me any questions they had. They recorded the session for future reference.

Her full name is Princess MisseySue, or Missey for short and, as soon as I started talking to her, she said, "I am so very thankful to them for allowing me my freedom. I never thought so much freedom was possible. It took me a long time to feel loved and not to be scared of the two-leggeds (humans). As Mom has noticed, sometimes I'm still bothered by my leg, especially in cold, humid weather. Mom likes to keep the windows of the house open all the time and sometimes it's chilly in the room and I do not like this." (They live close to the ocean.)

Millie asked her, "Do you want the windows closed?"

"Not all the time, just at night when it gets chilly."

MisseySue also talked about her stuffed toys and how much she loved the white one, more than any other color, but she was concerned because they didn't move. When Millie said she might be having a houseguest, MisseySue's first question was, "Will he move?"

We all laughed and said, "Yes."

When Rick asked, "Do you know you are loved?" Missey replied, "Yes. I always know when Dad comes home, and I always try to go out and say hi. I love his hands, so soft and loving. I have a special relationship with him and really love him."

When Millie asked if she liked to be cuddled and petted, Missey responded, "I don't like to be picked up and would much rather be on the floor and have you kneel down to give me some love."

Millie also wanted to know if Missey felt okay, or if she was sick or hurting anywhere. Missey replied that she felt very healthy. When asked what kind of food she wanted or craved, she said, "I like everything as long as it is crispy fresh. But I do have one craving."

Missey showed me a little bit of something wedged between two fingers that someone was offering to her. "It's something that I don't get very often because it's not good for me, but I want to tell them that I really like it."

I explained the picture as being of a light tan color and sweet smelling, and Rick said, "Oh, that's a banana. We try not to give her too much fruit but we know she loves it."

Missey went on, "The fireplace is my favorite place to be and I don't like it when someone is occupying my spot. Sometimes I just stare at them, or do other things to try to move them from there." Suddenly turning more serious, she said, "There's something else I need to say to them. When they were at the dinner table, I heard them talking about another rabbit that needs some help. If they are considering bringing him home [which later I found out they were], I am positive that I can be of help and would like to try to help him. I know what it is to be abused and could understand him and help him cope at first, then adapt to family life later. I would also like someone I can chase. Also, I am very motherly and would groom him often."

This was important for both Rick and Millie to hear. I did not know this but MisseySue had been abused as a baby. They had to fix a broken leg before adopting her. She was telling them she had experience because they were considering adopting a male rabbit with similar problems. He'd also been abused and had recently suffered a broken leg as well. After being operated on to fix the broken leg, he was being fostered but needed a permanent home. They were considering the possibilities and logistically how they were going to house the rabbits separately.

MisseySue and Sir Winston P. Bear

It was an eye-opening experience when their rabbit gave them, before even being asked, the okay to adopt another one.

They had known about this other rabbit and had been asked to foster him for a while, but Rick had reservations. What if the other rabbit didn't get along with Missey? He didn't want to get fully invested and have things not work out. We talked about his feelings and the importance of giving someone a chance. Being a foster parent means offering a temporary home and he could try to do that first.

When we said goodbye, Rick said that maybe he would try it for a couple of weeks and if it seemed to be working, he would call me back again. I expected to hear from them soon.

Rabbits and a Love Story

It didn't take long for Rick and Millie to e-mail me for an appointment to meet the new arrival, Sir Winston P. Bear, and to talk to MisseySue again.

When I arrived, MisseySue was in her usual place in the kitchen, while Winston was in his long pen upstairs in their bedroom. Each of them had their own playtime with the parents, away from each other, and every evening for a period of about twenty minutes they would all meet in the hallway (neutral territory), where neither of them was allowed on their own so as to avoid marking. There, under the supervision of Millie and Rick, they started to know each other by smelling and playing together.

We went downstairs into the living room and I asked Millie and Rick who they wanted to talk to first, but they didn't care. As soon as I closed my eyes, Missey began, "I want them to know that I am happy that they took my request seriously to help another rabbit in need and that it happened so fast. I also want them to know that even though Winston will eventually be my playmate, I consider myself the owner and master of this household, and it's up to me to let him know this. It will be on my terms, and no one else's. Winston will have to adjust to my rules and I will say when he is ready to join the household. In the meantime, I like the idea of having 'dates' every evening until I get to know him better. Both of us need time to adjust to one another and, even though I consider this arrangement similar to an arranged marriage, I need the opportunity to do it slowly and again on my terms.

"I worry that I feel cranky some days, very much like human females with PMS, and attribute this discomfort to my shedding hair [called 'molting' by those in the know]. It bothers me as I feel cranky and out of sorts. I ask them to be patient and not take it personally. It only lasts for a short while and usually goes away once I am involved in something very interesting, like going on my date."

On the subject of Winston, she said, "When I first saw him, he looked to me like Adonis. [We all laughed at this comparison but, in

Rabbits and a Love Story

fact, Winston is all white and double her size.] I am sometimes a little afraid of him because of his size. Sometimes I recoil and try to be careful, since he can be rough with me. He needs to understand that I need time and patience, and I need him to be softer. But I will always let him know when I think he is being too rough."

When asked about a change of food, she said, "I like it, especially those tidbits are good."

I said to Millie and Rick, "She is showing me some small shoots."

"Oh yes, we're feeding her alfalfa sprouts."

Missey was done with all her questions and answers, so I turned to Sir Winston P. Bear. When I tried to call him, his first response was, "I am confused about my name and need clarification before we talk."

Millie and Rick explained that he'd had a different name while at the shelter and they'd since changed it. Still confused, Winston said, "But they call me different names."

"Yes," Millie agreed. "I call him Winnie but I'm trying to be proper and call him Winston. Rick calls him P. Bear, so no wonder the guy is confused."

Still, he accepted the explanation in good humor and said, "I like the sound of 'Sir' in my name and having so many names makes me feel special. I will go along with the different names."

With that cleared up, he started. "I feel good in this house. Before I was in a household that treated me well and loved me very much but I didn't feel at home. [He was talking about another foster home.] But just a few hours after I arrived here, I felt that I belonged. I knew it felt right.

"I want Mom and Dad to know that I am thankful to them. I know they are trying their best to make me feel at home and I promise I'll try to be a good rabbit for them. I enjoy running around the circle. [He showed me an image of him running around the bed in a kind of frenzy until he's exhausted.] Exercising is good for me, otherwise I'll become very fat and that's no good. If I remain always in the den, my tummy tends to get upset for lack of movement and I get loose bowels. I love the smell of grass and I'm a digger, too. I would like to have an outing every once in a while.

"Please tell Mom how much I appreciate her caress. Before I used to be picked up by my ears and did not like that. It took me a while to understand that Mom pats my ears and gently separates them with a finger to caress them. I was apprehensive in the beginning, but am learning now how to enjoy it.

"I adore Princess MisseySue. I never had the opportunity to be close to a female rabbit before and didn't know until I was taken to the shelter that so many existed. I know I have some rough edges but am eager to play with her. I must learn to go easy and am trying to pay more attention. But I love the idea of having someone to share, to run and play with, and to love."

Suddenly, he fired an image at me of the future in which both rabbits were grooming each other and telling me that this was their goal. (As a note for those concerned about such things, both rabbits were fixed, so we were not being matchmakers to make babies here, just love.)

A couple of weeks later, I received an e-mail:

May 19

I just wanted you to know that Princess Missey is teaching us exactly what she meant about allowing her to take care of things, and teach Sir Winston!

She is doing VERY well, as is he! What special little people we are lucky enough to share our lives with! It has been with your help, education, and love that wonderful doors have been opened to all of us, and for this you have our deepest thanks, admiration, and love. You are as much a part of their lives as we!

Monica, thank you for being you, and for being open to the wonderful gifts you have been given, and for your willingness to share them and teach others about them—you are truly a gift to all of us!

May 28

We haven't forgotten about you. They had their first "sleep-over" together last night and did really really well! And guess what? Missey was the first to "give in."

She just couldn't stand it anymore and, the other day, they were both acting goofy, so I sent Missey to her room. When I went to put her gate up, who was sitting at the door? Sir Winston! I asked if he wanted to go in with his Missey (they had been in her room with the gate up before) and he ran right in and got "busy."

I put the gate up. He came and asked to have the gate down a couple of times, and I just told him that he had made the decision to go in with His Miss, and they could come back out in a while—they just needed to "cool their jets." He accepted that and went on with his business.

I came back about 45 minutes later to let them out, and he was "crashed out" on her bed! I went to open the gate and Missey, of course, was right there. She came out—he didn't want to move! I told him he could come out whenever he was ready; he was extremely comfy!

Missey went in to talk with him a couple of times, and the second time, he sat up, stretched, and gave the biggest yawn I have ever seen—I thought he was going to inhale the entire kitchen! She left to crash in the living room and he soon joined her. I went outside and told them, "Keep your bones calm. I'll be right back."

I was in the front courtyard, and got a sense that something was going on. I went back in and found my Precious Princess

Rabbits and a Love Story

drowning her Sir in big wet kisses! I think she just couldn't stand it any longer! Ergo, momma finally gave in and they were together all last night—they even "greeted" their first mutual "company" together while they were out running about! :)

Missey's a bit annoyed that Winnie's potty habits have gone down the tubes . . . but we're working on that one!

Thanks to our extended family member, YOU, we are achieving a VERY, VERY happy family here at the Carlton household! If we can just convince Winnie not to piddle all over the kitchen and perhaps give Missey kisses back, all will be right with the world!

Thank you so much for being the special person you are and for listening with your heart! :)

Update: June

The Miss and the Sir seem to be getting along quite well—they are now sleeping together (since last Thursday). I don't think there's much "sleeping" occurring—Missey is absolutely exhausted!

We would like to schedule a time next week or the week following, to have you come back down for some "chatter."

Missey has been smothering Winnie in BIG kisses since early last week, and Winnie has just, in the last couple of days, begun reciprocating! Now if we can just get back to the litter box and convince him that he doesn't have to piddle on Missey, I think we'll have it made! Anything you may be able to tell us and any suggestions you may have would be wonderful!

Thank you again for everything and for just being you!

On July 13 I went to see the Carlton gang again. It was great to be back. I went to the kitchen to get some water and was loudly complaining about my terrible experience with Southern California freeways. Suddenly, I became aware that Sir Winston had retreated to the farthest corner of the room. "You are too loud," he said. I laughed and told Millie.

The first one to speak was, as always, Missey who, in her unequivocal style, yelled, "Well, I can tell you one thing: the honeymoon is over!"

All of us roared in uncontrollable laughter. "So like her to say that," Rick said. "Missey is always unpredictable. She can be sweet, possessive, determined, motherly, and have the ultimate wisdom, but she's always unpredictable."

Then we started in with the questions. "Do you like the new litter?" Millie asked.

"It's okay, but I like the other one, too."

"Why are you guys peeing outside the box?" Millie continued.

"Well, he started it," Missey said. "I just do what he is doing. He is telling me I am his. I am telling him *no way.*"

"Do you want the litter box in a different place?" Millie asked.

"Yes, I like it where it was before he came. I need to be able to get in at the sides, and they are blocked by his box. Can you move it farther away, so that I can get into it better?"

"Would you like us to move his box to one side?"

"Put his all the way to the other corner."

"How are you doing?"

"I've been kind of fussy lately. Too hot, I guess," Missey admitted.

Rick asked, "Do you have enough room?" (I had to repeat the question out loud to make sure I understood it, and he verified that that was the question he wanted to ask.)

Missey responded, "You mean if I have enough room when you close the door to the kitchen and he is all over me, and we hardly have enough space to move, *nooo*," she shouted.

We all laughed again. This was Missey at her best. "Other than that," she continued, "when I have space to run around the living room area and feel free to do what I like, I am in control and happy."

With Winston we had a somewhat more relaxed conversation. "Winston, are you used to your new house?" asked Millie.

"I am so happy to be here. I never knew that I could have such a good relationship with a female. I worship her. She is the best. She's taught me so much that I do not know how to thank her enough. I like the fact that I now have a family. I enjoy being here now."

"How are you doing with the heat?"

"I like the frozen water bottle very much. It makes me feel good when I sit next to it."

"Do you like your new food?"

"For me food is not really that important. I take my time eating it but everything is yummy. Besides, whatever I don't eat, Missey will eat, and that makes me happy."

We talked about treats that both of them get and how Sir Winston eats the carrots but leaves the carrot top (the best part) for Missey.

As I was leaving, Winston sat next to the water bottle at first, then moved over to Missey and, as if showing off for my benefit, gave her a few kisses on the nose. Then they both snuggled close to each other. Missey closed her eyes approvingly and they both settled down.

As of this writing, more than a year and a half has passed. The two abused orphans have found each other and a family who makes them happy. This is far more than just a rabbit love story, however. The love that Millie and Rick have for their two "kids" exceeds that of many parents for their own children, and it's a love that is returned many-fold. The considerate way they introduced the two bunnies was rewarded by the stable bond that occurred.

CHAPTER 11

Mane Tales

Horses, I've read, have the understanding of a two-year-old child. Growing up with Mr. Ed, I wanted to believe that they were all like him, wise beyond human understanding, able to counsel us in time of need. As a child, I did not have the opportunity to be around horses. In fact, I was apprehensive of them. I never had riding lessons but enjoyed it when I tried it. Except for the soreness I experienced the next day, it was a lot of fun.

I once watched an episode of *That's Incredible* where a horse and its rider had a special relationship. The human was wheelchair-bound and the only freedom he could experience was on horseback. Only then did he feel like a full human being. The horse knew at some level how important it was for his human friend to ride him, so he would kneel down like a camel and lie on his side so that his rider could get in the saddle. Then, swiftly, he got up on all fours and rode into the wind. The story was touching and I wondered about the communication that took place between them.

Later, when I started to practice animal communication, I realized that horses had very real feelings and were able to express them through picture telepathy. But to what extent, I wondered. And how can they know the things they say?

These answers are still a mystery to me. Along the way, I have found that they do know more than us—sometimes more than their own doctors, as the next story illustrates.

Piñon Tosca

I was called in to talk to Piñon Tosca, a twelve-year-old mare with a damaged ligament in her right hind leg. Because the stables were hard to find, I went first to the owner's home and followed her by car to the stables.

The stables housed many horses, some outside grazing with ample grounds. Each had a designated roofed stall with hay on the ground. I parked and followed the owner, Mrs. Long, to where Stephanie, her daughter, had just finished giving Tosca a bath, and was grooming her.

They had bought the horse about a year ago and hadn't changed her name. The Spanish name translates to both "hard as a nut" and "stubborn as a rock." Both of them fit Tosca well.

She was stunning (see photograph, page 158). The day was cloudy but even without sunshine her coat, still a little wet, shone brilliantly.

She was still cross-tied after her bath and was waiting to dry off. She was huge, with long silky legs and an auburn mane that flowed softly to one side of her long neck. Her long tail flicked softly from side to side.

As always, before I see any of my clients, I had been communicating with Tosca all morning, telling her how important it was for her family to know just what she felt.

I said "hi" to Tosca as Stephanie dried her off. Tosca smelled me and allowed me to caress her face, a comforting feeling for both of us. She especially liked a certain spot under her lower lip to be rubbed. Tosca continued to allow me to do this while I talked with mother and daughter. I was careful to stay in her sight and not make any sudden moves. I could tell that she was comfortable being next to me. Suddenly her eyes widened at the sight of two magnificent horses, one being led to her stall and the other in the ring, running and playing. She became a little jealous, saying, "They are so beautiful. Look at them, they move like the wind."

After Stephanie had finished grooming her, we moved to her stall for a little privacy. We all got in and closed the gate behind us. I started by teaching Mom and Stephanie a little about communication and how it is done. All this time, Tosca stood in front of us, nuzzling my face and hair. I playfully responded by caressing her face and laughing at her antics. We didn't have anywhere to sit, so I leaned comfortably against the back of the gate for support. I turned on my tape machine and began. (I sometimes record the sessions for me as well as for my clients. If I am called in for something difficult or out of the ordinary, I want to be able to refer back to it at a later date. Sometimes my clients miss vital information and request to get a copy. This time I had a feeling that our conversation would turn out to be special, but didn't know just how special.)

Tosca was still in front of my face, perhaps two inches away, and very eager to talk. Knowing that I could "listen" to what she needed to say, she immediately said, "It was a stupid accident. It should not have

Piñon Tosca

After our session, top, and with her new foal, Skye, bottom.

happened. I am not in pain but know I need to rest the leg. I absolutely love to jump, and maybe I will be able to do that again."

"How long do you feel you need to heal completely?" I asked.

"A good six months."

Mom later told me, "Tosca's veterinarian said that this kind of injury can't heal and will be like that forever. He recommended that Tosca stop jumping and running, and instead concentrate on being a mother and maybe a show horse."

When Mom asked whether Tosca would be willing to have a baby and become a mother, she replied, "Even though I do not like babies belonging to others, I believe I would be a good mother to my own. But I want to be involved in the selection process because I am picky about finding the right male. I enjoy beauty and know that I am beautiful to look at. But I do not like to be compared to other beauties, as it makes me insecure."

When Tosca sent me this message in pictures, I saw the two females she'd been looking at before, one black and the other dark brown. I felt her admiration for their stance and coloring. She herself was a lighter chestnut brown but indeed very beautiful.

Tosca continued, "I am really happy here because everyone is kind and caring. This is a much better place than the one I had before. Tell Stephanie we understand each other at a deep level and that I'm thrilled that she allowed me to jump, even though it was not what she originally wanted to do. Maybe after I have my baby, I will learn to be still for a longer period of time, so that Stephanie can investigate other avenues of sharing our lives instead of jumping."

After I relayed this to Stephanie, Tosca changed the subject. "The evenings are getting cold and that really affects my leg. Could she wrap my leg to avoid the cold air making it stiff in the mornings?"

Stephanie said she would take care of that.

All during this time, Tosca had been next to me, nuzzling me gently at times, smelling my hair and my face and enjoying every minute of our talk. Both mom and daughter were surprised by her behavior. Stephanie said, "Tosca does not usually like people, and with anyone else she would have been in the corner of her pen, just munching hay. But not today."

Mom added, "I've never been able to touch or pet her because she always moves away from me."

I conveyed this to Tosca and, for the first time, she allowed Mom to pet her head. They were astonished at the obvious results and I was delighted at the outcome. But I was to be even more surprised when, a few months later, I received this note:

Dear Dr. Monica,

I wanted you to know Tosca and Stephanie showed this weekend. They were wonderful. Tosca was so frisky. She knew Stef and her trainer are keeping an eye on her leg. So far so good. We may have ultrasound again.

There will be another show at the Oaks in San Juan (a well-known facility in San Juan Capistrano in Southern California). I will let you know when. I would love for you to see them in action. Perhaps if you are in the area that weekend you could come watch. I took some photos. Enjoy!

P.S. It's been only five months since Tosca got hurt and yet she won second and third placements without being pushed.

The photographs clearly show Tosca jumping obstacles in great form, both rider and horse in perfect sync. Despite the fact that her doctor had said she would never completely heal, after only five months, she could jump again! Tosca really knew best!

Jack and Rooster

Recently, I spoke with a horse whose mom, Becky, had contacted me by e-mail. She was concerned about her horse because he was getting old, and wanted to find out if he would be receptive to getting a younger companion.

The old horse was Jack, a Tennessee Walker about twenty-five years old. In our session, he told Becky, "We have been through thick and thin together. There have been many good times, and always I was able to feel your love for me. I used to be quite handsome, you know," he said as a side comment to me.

"Now my back has bowed down a bit. I can still trot and I do a good job. I will not feel bad about adding a new member to our family. In fact, we horses are very family-oriented. I hope the new boy is good-natured. I would like to teach him a thing or two, if he is willing. You have to be very patient around here, and he probably does not know how yet."

When Jack mentioned that he loves to hear Becky's voice and asked her not to stop talking to him, she replied, "I love talking to him but was wondering if maybe he thought it was too much."

Rooster was the name of the horse Becky had decided to buy. Also a Tennessee Walker, he was about two years old. She'd already e-mailed me with his photo and I could see how very beautiful this light tan horse was, with his white socks and long mane and tail. But what struck me most was his champion's stance. He still needed to undergo training and Becky could not take him home right away. She also did not like his name and wondered if she could change it.

Through me, Rooster told Becky, "I liked you very much the moment I met you."

"The admiration was mutual," she responded.

He said, "I am ready to work hard. I love excitement and to go places and to feel that I have a job and a purpose. I love children and find myself getting more attracted to women than men. I don't care too much for my name either. I need a name that captures my personality better, but I will leave it up to you."

Becky was torn between two names so we asked him which he preferred. "The first is Jessie," she said, which drew no response. But when she said "Shiloh," I immediately felt his acceptance and heard him comment, "The name has a sing-song quality to it that I really like. Yes, I like the sound of it, so Shiloh it is!"

Shiloh added, "I like the idea of having a big brother and will be good. I'm looking forward to going to my new home."

A few months later, when Becky brought Shiloh home, she later told me that as soon as he was free in the paddock, she called out "Shiloh!" and he immediately came trotting over to her!

"Amazing," she said. "I would not have believed that a new horse could be so aware and responsive to his new name if it hadn't happened to me."

Mister and Corinda

Linda called me to have a consultation with Mister, her gelding of twenty years. I was also there to see Corinda, her sixteen-year-old mare.

It was unusual to hear a warning: "Mister had a consultation with another communicator a few years back, and he didn't like her at all. For the first time in his life he charged someone, baring his teeth, and was ready to attack her. I had to stop him. He might not be happy to see you. But I need to talk to him! Could you give it a try?"

I arrived at Linda's home ready for a rough encounter. I was cautious. We paced the arena and settled at the gate for a chat. I was prepared with a bribe: huge, fresh carrots were coming out of my bag every time Mister would approach, so he felt comfortable right away. Corinda was right next to him and enjoyed some of the carrots too.

Mister told us he was not happy with his living arrangements and most of all was missing his time to play with his mom. Linda told me that they had recently moved to the present home and she had been busy with the move and hadn't ridden him in over a month.

Mister also complained repeatedly of how boring this new place was. The new home was in an area that was very quiet, with hardly any homes around it, and he found himself with nothing to do and no distractions either. He talked about missing his friends and later Linda commented that he had been boarded. He described what his favorite living arrangements would be like and requested more interaction from her.

When Linda asked to know what was his favorite saddle, Mister not only described the saddle but the color, the texture of it next to his skin, and how much more comfortable were the belts under his belly.

Mister was so taken by my gift of carrots that he stayed by my side during the whole hour we talked, sniffing at my hair and placing his big face next to mine. He hugged me many times!

Mom was ecstatic. I was delighted!

Corinda was shy and introverted. She was very fearful of everything and hadn't been able to ride her new trail at all. She was jumpy and would run back home at the slightest sound.

Corinda's consultation was very moving because she was able to explain something that had happened when she was very young. She remembered being outside, galloping in the fields on a wet, damp morning with a little girl on her back. The dirt was muddy and the girl wanted to go fast. They were going through an unfamiliar area when all of a sudden Corinda stopped dead in her tracks. She had seen an opening in the ground and what looked like an exposed piece of pipe. Because of the sudden move, the little girl flew out of her saddle, went over her head, and landed on the ground. Corinda knew that she was at fault and never forgave herself for hurting the little girl. She was punished, too, she said. She was not allowed to run with her little mistress anymore. Instead, she was kept for breeding purposes only and not very loved or cared for.

Linda explained that Corinda was found outside exposed to inclement weather conditions and famished. In her new home with Linda, she's treated very well. Notwithstanding, every time she is taken for a ride she still has the feeling that she might do something wrong and gets so scared she just wants to come back home, where it is safe.

The feeling of having done something wrong was so strong that it prompted me to ask Linda if anything unusual had happened lately.

Linda said that Corinda was on the trail while her husband was riding her when all of a sudden, and apparently for no reason, she had stopped her canter and thrown him off her back.

Corinda then said she was concerned with what kind of punishment she would get now and wanted us to tell her dad how very sorry she was. Linda told her that Dad was not blaming her for his fall at all but Corinda could not believe us. She was reading Dad's pictures (in his mind) every time he came near her. She knew that the fall was always in the back of his mind.

An arrangement was made to begin the long process of recovery, and Linda and her husband are working things out. Corinda is being walked on the trail until she feels more comfortable and is making progress. Dad is trying to picture in his mind a happy Corinda who loves to walk on the trail as he is working on not being fearful, and a horse trainer is also helping a few times a week.

Linda was very pleased with the results of this consultation because it has given her a new understanding of both her horses and how to help them live a happy life.

The Wild Ones

$\int$ ome animals have been domesticated for many thousands of years. Others, such as cats, have been domesticated for only about 4,000 years. Still, even as a species, some cats will forever be wild. Take, for instance, feral cats born and raised without human touch, not relying on humans for nourishment or company. What happens when you try to bring a wild cat into your home? Do they ever lose their aggression or fear of people?

Most of the time they don't, unless the kitten is very young and able to learn to trust humans. Of course, this is a generalization, but if you try to bring an older feral cat into your home, he will have a hard time blending in with others for the rest of his life. Still, I have found that if I try to talk to them, they can reason just as well as a domesticated animal. The difference is that they are so surprised you are actually talking with them that they don't know quite how to respond, as in the first story.

Sam

Norma called me into her home because one of her cats, Minue, was missing and the other cat, as well as she, was traumatized by his absence. In my mind, I went searching for Minue and he sent me pictures of himself close to some railroad tracks, scared and hiding from a coyote he had seen nearby. When he described the area, Norma knew exactly where he was and went off to retrieve him.

Norma shared a huge house with eight resident cats plus two outside tenants who would come around at feeding time. She told me, "One of the eight residents was once feral. I took him in after he'd been in a fight and gotten badly hurt. After healing, he became dependent on me for food and decided to adopt me. I named him Sam and today he's about ten. I wanted you to see him because he's developed a mouth infection that stops him from eating normally. He foams at the mouth and drools constantly. I often find him sitting in front of the food bowl just looking at it, unable to swallow."

Sam, a large black male, was out on the light and airy covered patio surrounded by all kinds of cat toys, carpeted cat trees, high shelves, cozy beds, litter boxes, and places to hide.

When Norma asked me to talk to him and see what I could do, I was apprehensive. As I approached the patio, he immediately went up to the rafters to hide from us. Norma took a long time to convince him to come down and when he did, he dashed into the house and hid under the bed in the spare room. We followed him in and closed the door and window. We pulled up the bed skirts on the side of the bed, Norma on one side and me on the other. Sam was squeezed all the way to the back wall and no amount of coaxing would bring him out. I tried everything I could think of to communicate to him that I meant him no harm. He refused, saying, "Go away."

Finally, after much trying, he got so upset with us that he tried to run out of the room but was met with a closed door and four hands. He stopped dead in his tracks, long enough for us to grab him. I wanted to see inside his mouth but Norma said, "You won't be able to do it. Even I can't touch him. I warn you, he'll bite."

I decided that Sam needed a little healing instead of talking. Talk could come later. While I sent him pictures of well-being and love, I began the healing. I started slowly touching him on the back and very slowly moving my hand, alternating sides in slow round movements. After about five minutes, I got to his face. All this time, Norma had been holding him down. In the beginning, he fought her, but he had now relaxed and was just waiting to see what would happen.

We could tell he was beginning to enjoy himself because he had crouched down on the carpet in a sitting/resting position, his tail completely relaxed and his eyes half-closed. Always on the alert, however, he would not allow himself to lose control, so his eyes would open again. As I sent healing energy to the area around his mouth, I slowed down the movements of my hand to a slight touch, using my fingertips to barely touch the area of his mouth. He exhibited no sign of aggression, so I continued. I was able to touch both sides of his mouth and the top of his nose, very sensitive areas for all cats, and especially for Sam, who'd never been touched there before.

I told Norma, "Relax your grip on him and then slowly move one of your hands and touch his face as I'm doing."

With my hand on top of hers, I showed her how to continue the healing. Because I'd begun talking out loud, Sam lost his concentration so I decided it was time to quit. I completed the healing by directing Norma on how to touch him on both cheeks for a few more seconds. Finally, I asked Norma to release the hand that was still holding him.

Sam was obviously enjoying this treatment since, when we were finished, he stayed there without needing to be held down. He looked at me and then at Norma and said, "That was nice."

Then he turned around and, after Norma opened the window, disappeared back to the patio. Norma was in heaven. "In all the years I've had him," she said, "I was never able to touch him like today!"

I set up a healing schedule for Sam and Norma, who promised to follow up with his treatment.

She said she would call me next time Sam started to drool over his food but, since she hasn't, I am assuming that all is well.

Kayenta

One of my wild animal cases involved Kayenta, the dog of a friend and fellow teacher named Isa. Being part coyote, Kayenta had a distinctive appearance and her wild instincts would be with her for the rest of her life.

Raising Kayenta proved hard. She had an instinctual habit that Isa could never train out of her: she attacked anything smaller than herself. She was also very hesitant in accepting strangers. She did not like other people or animals, only Isa, who called me in for a consultation when Isa gave birth to twins. Knowing Kayenta's attitude toward children, Isa was keeping Kayenta from coming into the house and seeing the babies, and wanted to explain things to her. She especially wanted Kayenta to know how much she loved her, as they had been inseparable before the babies were born.

Kayenta was not a happy dog. "I'm sad that my status as the first and only companion has been threatened. Now that the babies are here, I'm not even allowed in the house anymore. I spend the whole day outside on the little patio with no yard, flies swarming around me, and I'm becoming a vegetable. I'm losing my appetite and am hot and angry. I came into this world for a purpose, and that purpose has been fulfilled. I'm supposed to teach Isa how to handle unruly kids by being one myself. [Isa is a grade-school teacher.] I also taught Isa how to handle her own family. And now that she finally has one, she sees no more reason for keeping me around. I just want out."

Isa asked Kayenta, "Would you rather go up into the hills and be free?"

Kayenta replied, "I know I'm a good hunter, but I don't know what freedom is about. [Though part coyote, she had never lived in the wild.] I don't really know if I would be okay on my own even though I can find shelter and have always been a good hunter."

Isa was torn and asked Kayenta, "Would you really rather go into the spirit world and be free of all worries? I want to do whatever's the best thing for you."

Because Isa did not want to believe that Kayenta was telling her that she wanted to release her body, she continued to ask Kayenta, "Would you rather find a new home with someone else?"

Kayenta was adamant. "I am used to being around only you, Mom, so how could I possibly get used to someone else? You know better than that!" she snapped. She promised Isa a sign that would demonstrate how she truly wanted to go back to Spirit: she would be very good at the vet, behaving as she had never done before.

Isa was stumped. She could not put Kayenta to sleep without first checking out all the other alternatives. She called all the shelters, the Humane Society, and Wild Animal Rescue, but none would take a hybrid animal. Isa was at her wits' end but it took her two more months to bring herself to put Kayenta to sleep.

By then, Kayenta was turning on everyone, first Isa's husband and then even Isa herself. No one could come close to her and even feeding time was risky, involving going out to the patio, putting down her food, and leaving swiftly before she could get close enough to bite. When she attempted to attack a child who had come over to play (but was prevented from doing so by a sliding glass door), Isa realized it was time. After much praying, Isa finally made the dreaded phone call for an appointment with her vet.

At my guidance, Isa talked with Kayenta about the procedure and told her that she was just doing what Kayenta wanted. That morning, Kayenta walked happily to the car, wagging her tail, staying still on the ride to the vet's office without her customary barking out the window. Once there, she greeted the receptionist and the vet by wagging her tail without a single bark, and lay down on the floor for her lethal injection.

She clearly understood the situation and Isa's heart was not quite so broken, knowing that she was doing what her friend wanted. Being released in this way was the best thank-you Kayenta could have ever hoped for. Isa knelt by her side until her friend's breathing stopped. She stroked her fur one last time, said a prayer, and cried until she had no more tears left. Kayenta was finally at peace.

Two days later, Isa was walking along the creek where she and Kayenta used to walk in the mornings. Laying on the path were two white feathers. She knew it was a sign from Kayenta. Now, as the twins are growing, Isa has realized that Kayenta was preparing her for one child, who definitely does not fit into "business as usual," much like Kayenta was. With this knowledge she knows that Kayenta is, on some level, still with her.

Tasha

I love being called in for something different. When Patty called me in to see her wolf, she wanted to know how much experience I'd had with wild animals. "It doesn't matter," I said. "Even with a lot of experience, the knowledge that we receive from them is always on an individual basis."

Tasha was a four-year-old female wolf with about 20 percent Siberian husky. She shared her life with Duke, a male Siberian husky of eleven years.

When I got to the house, Tasha was on the balcony and noticed me right away. As a greeting, she starting barking—well, actually, a howl and a bark rolled into one that echoed through the street and sounded quite intimidating.

The animals were not free to roam in the house, but were allowed into a side room with sofas and access to the patio.

Patty went in first and told Tasha that it was okay for me to enter her room. Tasha looked at me and assumed a position of command. She started to bark loudly and I became a little apprehensive even though I knew I didn't have to be, for I felt no attack thoughts from her. Very slowly, I knelt on the floor, crossed my hands over my chest in a gesture of submission, lowered my head and did not look at her. This was intended to put her at ease, as a non-threatening, non-dominating pose, a kind of calming signal. It also piqued her curiosity about me, so she slowly approached and I allowed her to smell me from head to toe. My only movement was breathing and, even then, I tried to do that gently. I emptied my mind of any fearful thought and concentrated instead on a loving greeting.

Tasha was huge, much larger than her male companion, and towered over my slight frame. I didn't want to think that, at any time, she could snap and really injure me. Instead, I felt confident that I was there to help her and to talk to her. She seemed to receive my advances well. When she was certain that she knew my various smells, she calmed down. Then Patty, her husband, Tom, and I sat down on the sofas. Tasha sat on the floor while Duke, the male husky, kept going between the patio and the room.

Tasha began by telling me how she loved being out on the patio, looking up to the night, and having a long howl into the starry sky, her paws high on the fence. She felt great just hearing her own echo and knowing she was spreading her word out and that everyone could hear.

Her parents had several questions. "How about food, would you rather eat twice a day?"

"No," she said, "once in the morning is enough. But I really look forward to those cookies in the evening. I like to walk very much but wish I could go after prey."

Tom was concerned about letting her run free and said so. Tasha agreed. "I don't think I could control myself or pay attention to you if I were to roam free. My well-being and security come first. I am number one and need to take care of myself. Even though I love my family and would never do anything bad to them, I would do what I wanted to do first and if, at certain times, I didn't feel like obeying your commands to come, sit, or stay, I wouldn't pay any attention to them."

Patty and Tom laughed at this, knowing full well that Tasha had always had problems in accepting directions from them.

Tasha went on, "There are other things more important to me, like protecting the house, keeping an eye on the neighbors, preventing other dogs from soiling my territory, and overseeing family activities. These responsibilities prevent me from obeying silly commands like come and stay."

One of the things the parents needed to talk to Tasha about was her habit of chasing after cars. Tasha said, "I do not like anything that comes from behind me and can go faster than I can. My instinct is to run after whatever is going faster and gain on it, much as if it were prey."

As a form of behavior modification, I suggested to Tom, "Every time a car starts to pass you on the street, turn around and change directions so Tasha doesn't feel as if she has to follow the car. Fortunately you live in a cul-de-sac and not many cars drive by."

Patty next voiced a concern. "When I take them out for a walk, I have to take them one at a time because I can't handle both of them at the same time. Tasha is just too strong. But Tasha gets upset when it's

Duke's turn to go out for a walk; Tasha wants to go out, too. I think that Tasha is jealous."

Tasha replied, "You're wrong. I don't get upset because I am jealous of Duke. It's because I am concerned that Duke won't come back. I can't stand to be separated from him. I get an anxiety attack. I feel the same when Tom leaves."

Both Patty and Tom knew full well how very much attached Tasha was to Duke and were very concerned because Duke, at eleven years old, was slowing down and they feared the time when he would die and the effect this would have on Tasha. (Wolves mate for life.) Patty suggested, "Maybe we should bring a young male into the household before Duke goes to give Tasha enough time to get used to the new arrival."

Tasha explained, "I understand about death and agree that, being so attached to Duke, it will be terrible for me to lose him. But I can't even think of having another male in the house. So, no! Please do not bring another male dog into the house now."

Tom asked Tasha how she felt about the poodles across the street. "I do not like them one bit. They're always yapping and they think they are the best creatures in this world. I could show them a thing or two."

When Tom asked if she would hurt them if she got the chance, she immediately and without hesitation answered, "*Yes!*"

Tasha went on, "I must be allowed to be my own self. I am not a circus act. Therefore I will only accept directions when I feel they do not compromise any of my other actions."

When asked why she wouldn't go to the pool with Duke, who swims and loves the water, Tasha answered by showing me a pond. "Water is for drinking when you are thirsty. If there was prey in the water, I would go after it, but water is not for entertainment. I do not like it."

Tom asked her why, if she enjoys her trips in the car, she wouldn't go on the train?

"Because I don't like the high-pitched sound of the engine running or the vibration from the train and will not go on it."

"How about a boat ride?" Tom asked.

"A boat goes on water, doesn't it? I don't like it!" Tasha replied with an attitude.

Just then, Duke came in the living room and licked my hand. Patty said, "He looks like he wants to talk. Could you see if he wants to say anything?"

Duke was in awe that we could talk and decided he would like to give it a try. He sent me a few pictures of his life up until then, which I relayed to Patty and Tom. He mentioned how different Tasha was from Riva, another husky he knew. Duke added, "I am very happy with Tasha and she takes good care of me. Nothing bothers me and I love her very much. I heard Mom and Dad talking about me and the fact that I am old. Please ask them to keep me in the house for as long as they can so that Tasha can take good care of me until my last day."

They promised they would and he felt happy with that.

It was time for me to go and I stood up to leave. Tasha became angry and let me know it by growling deeply and standing erect two feet away from my face. Worried, Tom and Patty told her to back off. I understood perfectly, however, since this had been her first experience at talking. She was comfortable being able to express her feelings and wanted me to stay, so I told her out loud, "Okay, I'll stay a little longer."

As I slowly sat down, she relaxed as well and sat in front of me. Then, as if to thank me, she approached me and kissed me several times on my face (see photograph). Duke imitated her, approving of me as well. I sent Tasha images of my two little dogs at home waiting for me. She understood and backed off a few steps to give me room. As I left, Patty told me, "This has been the best experience of my life. Thank you so much. Your visit has brought us closer to our pets than we ever thought possible."

Tasha and Duke

For my part, I was in awe of the fierce courage, loyalty, and self-determination of the majestic Tasha. I will never look at a wolf quite the same after meeting her.

The next story is not really about a wild animal, although people feared him. He wasn't a hybrid, but was raised being allowed to act on instinct and impulse. Since I knew none of it at the time, I went to his home and greeted him in the same manner I do any of my dog clients, with an open heart and an open mind.

Magick and Morres

I met Morgan when I went to the store where she worked to do a pet consultation day. I later found out that she was a great teacher of metaphysics, giving classes every Monday night on different subjects, from meditation to Tarot. Morgan thought it would be great for her two dogs to have a consultation with me. Being a psychic herself, she could do a pretty good job of reading them but, as with doctors and psychiatrists, psychics also rely on others when it involves themselves and their families.

Because they are both rare breeds, I was excited to meet her dogs. Magick was a three-year-old male Belgian sheepdog (Groenendael) and Morres was a six-year-old male Belgian Malinois (see photograph).

As always happens, when I first walked in the door, Morres and Magick came to say hello. They were both huge and I am barely five feet tall, so they surrounded me and immediately started to smell me. I wasn't scared of them at all; they were obviously glad to meet me and I had already talked to them and explained why I was coming.

Morgan commented that they were behaving differently than usual. "Magick usually jumps all over people, while Morres stays put and guards."

Magick licked me for a while and then went outside to get a toy to bring to me. Morres went up the stairs a few steps and barked at Morgan, as if telling her something. Morgan stood in the middle of the hall, not believing her eyes and saying again, "I can't believe it. They usually do not behave this way with strangers. There is something different about today."

We moved into the living room, where Morgan recorded the session. We started with Magick, who said, "I am really happy that Morres is going back to work. I wasn't getting the attention I was used to."

This was an interesting piece of information because dogs do not tell me they "go to work" except on rare occasions when they need to accompany one of their guardians. (They do, however, talk a lot about their "jobs.")

Magick confirmed that his relationship with Morgan was very special and that they have a lot to learn from each other. I told Morgan,

Morres and Magick

"Magick feels just like a puppy or an overgrown adolescent, instead of an adult dog. His favorite thing is to cuddle up next to you, imagining he still fits on your lap."

The session continued with a lot of different questions, during which Magick sat down between the two of us. Because I had my eyes closed, I did not know where Morres was. When I started to talk with Morres, he immediately moved closer to me, putting his head on my lap and leaning his body next to mine. Two of his legs were positioned next to my left foot while his rump rested comfortably on my right foot. He was the perfect loving dog and acted as if we were best friends. He enjoyed the touch of my hand throughout our conversation. The first thing he said was, "I am also very happy to go back to work. I couldn't take it anymore, doing nothing around the house and getting fat."

Again, this "work" reference puzzled me but I didn't want to ask Morgan directly, especially knowing she was a psychic herself. I didn't want her to have any questions regarding the validity of what was coming through, but I was getting curious.

Morres's most interesting comment was directed to Morgan. "She should not worry about me spending time in my big crate. It's just fine for me. I need to be there so that I know I no longer need to listen for 'bad people.' I can relax there. Mom worries about me being in the crate, and I want to make sure that she doesn't, because it's fine with me."

Surprised at this, Morgan said, "That is one of my biggest worries. I'm very happy that he addressed that early on in our conversation. Does Morres know that Dad had an operation?"

Morres, who was very intelligent, said, "I consider Mom's husband to be my partner, not my dad. He's a very good and tough partner. I knew something was wrong a few days before he quit work because his behavior was different. He walked more slowly and stayed very close to me. I know when it's time to go to work in the mornings because my partner starts to dress, and I get very excited and can't wait until it's time to go."

Mom asked, "Why does he offer his paw to people, not to shake like other dogs, but for people to hold it?"

Morres gave me a picture of a lot of people in uniform lined up with their dogs next to them. One man stood in front, whom everyone respected. This man started at one end of the line and shook the hand of each man and patted the dogs. He called this "acceptance," and said, "I want to feel accepted."

Morgan asked, "Does he remember his training in Europe?"

Morres said, "Yes, I do," and sent me a picture of a lot of activity around him. I saw him learning how to run very fast at angles and also in circles, how to keep his balance and not fall down, and to attack and release on command. The images puzzled me and I wondered if they had anything to do with his "work."

The Wild Ones

"All my commands were given in Finnish so people don't think I can understand English. I want Mom to know that I understand very well what I'm told, that language is not really a barrier for me and, besides, Magick has taught me a few things, too. When I am home, I will obey my mom but, in any other setting, I am trained to obey only one person and that is my partner. I love my job and am happy when I come home to my family."

The session felt over, and Morgan explained, "Morres is a police canine. He was trained in Holland and came to the USA shortly after training, and was assigned to my husband, a police officer, as his partner. He is considered the most vicious police dog in the force. He always goes in first for the attack and needs to be stopped because he can rip off a man's arm. A lot of my friends refuse to come to the house for fear of Morres. When he comes home from a hard day at work fighting the 'bad people,' he goes to his large crate to sleep. Because my husband works nights, he needs to sleep during the daytime hours when Magick is just starting his day. I'm glad he understands that when he's in his crate, it's so he doesn't have to work and can rest and sleep while Magick takes care of the home. Because my husband needed an operation, Morres has been home for over a month. He knows his partner is up and around so they will soon be going back to work.

"In the morning, when my husband gets ready to go to work and puts his uniform on, it's time for Morres to go to work as well and he gets very excited to take on the day. Although only his partner can give him commands in Finnish, he will respect only those who deserve it. His present partner is the only one he will listen to and obey."

He may be the most ferocious dog in the county but, to me, he was a little puppy dog who stood on my feet and leaned against me with such love and affection that I would take him home with me any day.

Just before I left, to show his affection, Morres went out to get his favorite sock and brought it to me to play. It made a wonderful photo.

The Wild Ones

My conversations with hybrid, wild, and "ferocious" animals have convinced me that they are all able to relate their feelings and emotions to any given question. How could we possibly think of them as anything less than thinking beings?

In his book *Kinship with All Life*, J. Allen Boone writes about two chiefs, one an American Indian, the other a Bedouin of the Arabian desert. He wrote, "These two men living thousands of miles apart would naturally be considered complete aliens. Yet they share a common vision and move in almost precisely the same mental, spiritual and physical rhythms. Their lives are held together by the same golden thread.

"They connect with all animals by sending them feelings and pictures, and by relating to them as 'celestial creatures' or as 'rational fellow beings.' 'God,' they say, 'has in His infinite Wisdom, Power and Purpose pervaded the Universe, that wherever one looked he could always see God shining through all things, and hear Him speaking wisdom through all things.'

"There is, of course, nothing original in what the Bedouin and the Indian accomplished by recognizing animals as being on mental and spiritual communicating levels with themselves. Job recommended the same practice many centuries ago:

> Ask the very beasts, and they will teach you;
> Ask the wild birds—they will tell you;
> Crawling creatures will instruct you,
> Fish in the sea will inform you:
> For which of them all knows not that this is the Eternal's way,
> In whose control lies every living soul,
> And the whole life of man (Job 12:7–10)."

The Wild Ones

Epilogue

Over the years, I have spoken with countless animals, some alive, some crossed over. They have common denominators: they all give unconditional love, accept us the way we are, have great compassion, and are completely loyal.

I believe the future will see a lot of changes for the better concerning our animal friends as more and more of us treat them as part of the family. In my vision for the future, animals will no longer be used for medical research, clothing, or recycled as food. Stricter legislation will make dognapping and cruelty cases criminal offenses. I recall the news story in which a man in northern California threw a woman's fluffy little lapdog into traffic following a minor traffic incident, and was sentenced to three years in prison. While the crime stemmed from road rage and was appalling, I was pleased that the legal system also saw it that way, although nothing could bring the little dog back.

We will see regulations on spaying and neutering across the country. When you purchase an animal, it will need to be sterilized prior to going home with you, as some shelters are doing right now, specifically in California where such a law passed at the beginning of the new millennium. Hopefully, this will avoid the millions of animals a year that are euthanized now because they can't find a home. Special licenses will be issued for breeders, who will operate under strict supervision in order to eradicate puppy mills.

All pets will need to be licensed, whether a dog, cat, rabbit, iguana, bird, or horse. All will need some kind of identification that can't be removed, whether a microchip or retina identification or whatever new technology we can come up with.

Humans will no longer be referred to as "owners" but rather as guardians or companions of our pets. Animals will stop being property and start having some rights.

Education for humans on how to care for pets will become just as important as education for childcare. Daycare will be available where you leave your dogs while you go to work, so that they are not home alone. And workplaces will be more "dog friendly." This will reduce the number of animals needing medicine for separation anxiety and other behaviors related to boredom like excessive barking, chewing, and digging.

Dog walkers and pet sitters will be trained in proper animal care and CPR, and special classes will be available through high school courses and adult education classes. Enclosed parks and special stretches of beaches will be safe havens for those humans who like to take their animal companions on outings.

Seat belts will eventually become mandatory for pets. Otherwise a carrier will be required. No more riding in the backs of pickup trucks or jumping out of open windows!

Pets will be allowed in all sidewalk cafes and restaurants with outside patios, as they are right now in parts of Europe. People will know they have to pick up after their animals or otherwise be fined. And pet health insurance will be as common as for humans.

Technology will be available to cure animals at the same pace as humans. For a nominal fee, euthanasia will be available when an animal is suffering from an incurable disease. We will see more pet cemeteries and more cremations done for pets. We will see more memorials, religious or otherwise, where we can celebrate their life and mourn openly.

Cruelty for sport or pleasure, such as dog and bullfights, cockfighting, and fox hunting will be unthinkable and prohibited by law, with penalties as severe as for cruelty to humans.

Finally, more dogs will work in all areas of life, such as medical assistance, therapy, search and rescue, and sniffing for termites, drugs, or drug money.

We will learn from our animals to commune with nature and to work with all our senses—to smell the wind, hear the water, taste the rain, feel the moon, and see the spirits. We will be certain, no matter what our religious belief, that there is no heaven if our animal friends are not there with us.

In the meantime, let us continue to give them a place in our homes and in our hearts. Let us continue to try to improve our communication skills and maybe one day we will be able to speak to them just as our ancestors did.

I hope that the stories in this book have opened your mind a little to the rich inner world of our pets and helped you look at your companions with new eyes. They are far from "dumb animals" and have much to share "for those with eyes to see and ears to hear."

Epilogue

Recommended Reading

Boone, J. Allen. *Kinship with All Life*. Harper Collins, 1954.

Camuti, Luis J., D.V.M. *All My Patients Are Under the Bed*. Simon and Schuster, 1985.

Emoto, Masaru. *The Hidden Messages in Water*. Beyond Words Publishing, 2004.

Estés, Clarissa Pinkola, Ph.D. *Women Who Run with the Wolves*. Ballantine Books, 1992.

Frazier, Anitra. *The New Natural Cat: A Complete Guide for Finicky Owners*. Dutton Books, 1990.

Gallegos, Eligio. *The Personal Totem Pole: Animal Imagery, the Chakras and Psychotherapy*. Moon Bear Press, 1990.

Grandin, Temple. *Thinking In Pictures and Other Reports from My Life with Autism*. Vintage Books, 1995.

Griscom, Chris. *The Healing of Emotion: Awakening the Fearless Self*. Light Institute Press, 1999.

Harris, Julia. *Pet Loss: A Spiritual Guide*. Lantern Books, 2002.

Hearne, Vicki. *Animal Happiness*. Harper Collins, 1994.

Kubler-Ross, Elisabeth. *On Death and Dying*. Collier Books, 1969.

Loeb, Paul and Suzanne Hlavacek. *Smarter Than You Think*. Pocket Books, 1997.

Masson, Jeffrey Moussaieff and Susan McCarthy. *When Elephants Weep: The Emotional Lives of Animals*. Delacorte Press, 1995.

Masson, Jeffrey Moussaieff. *Dogs Never Lie About Love*. Crown Publishers, 1997.

McElroy, Susan. *Animals As Teachers and Healers: True Stories and Reflections*. New Sage Press, 1996.

Morgan, Marlo. *Mutant Message Down Under*. MM Co., 1991.

Myers, Arthur. *Communicating with Animals: The Spiritual Connection Between People and Animals*. Contemporary Books, 1997.

Pitcairn, Richard H., D.V.M. and Susan Hubble Pitcairn. *Dr. Pitcairn's Complete Guide to Natural Health for Dogs and Cats*. Rodale Press, Inc., 1995.

Recommended Reading

Quackenbush, Jamie and Denise Graveline. *When Your Pet Dies: How to Cope with Your Feelings.* Simon and Schuster, 1985.

Randour, Mary Lou. *Animal Grace: Entering a Spiritual Relationship with Our Fellow Creatures.* New World Library, 2000.

Schoen, Allen M. *Kindred Spirits: How the Remarkable Bond Between Humans and Animals Can Change the Way We Live.* Broadway Books, 2002.

Scully, Matthew. *Dominion: The Power of Man, the Suffering of Animals, and the Call to Mercy.* St. Martin's Griffin, 2003.

Smith, Penelope. *Animal Talk: Interspecies Telepathic Communication.* Beyond Words Publishing, 1999.

Stein, Diane. *The Holistic Puppy.* Crossing Press, 1998.

———. *The Women's Book of Healing: Auras, Chakras, Laying On of Hands, Crystals, Gemstones, and Colors.* Ten Speed Press, 2004.

———. *The Women's Spirituality Book (Llewellyn's New Age Series).* Llewellyn, 1986.

Tellington-Jones, Linda. *The Tellington T-Touch.* Penguin Books, 1992.

Weaver, Helen. *The Daisy Sutra.* Buddha Rock Press, 2000.

Wylder, Joseph. *Psychic Pets: The Secret Life of Animals.* Gramercy Books, 1978.

LLEWELLYN ORDERING INFORMATION

Order Online:
Visit our website at www.llewellyn.com, select your books, and order them on our secure server.

Order by Phone:
- Call toll-free within the U.S. at 1-877-NEW-WRLD (1-877-639-9753). Call toll-free within Canada at 1-866-NEW-WRLD (1-866-639-9753)
- We accept VISA, MasterCard, and American Express

Order by Mail:
Send the full price of your order (MN residents add 7% sales tax) in U.S. funds, plus postage & handling to:

Llewellyn Worldwide
P.O. Box 64383, Dept. 0-7387-0629-9
St. Paul, MN 55164-0383, U.S.A.

Postage & Handling:
Standard (U.S., Mexico, & Canada). If your order is:
$49.99 and under, add $3.00
$50.00 and over, FREE STANDARD SHIPPING

AK, HI, PR: $15.00 for one book plus $1.00 for each additional book.

International Orders (airmail only):
$16.00 for one book plus $3.00 for each additional book

Orders are processed within 2 business days.
Please allow for normal shipping time. Postage and handling rates subject to change.

Is Your Pet Psychic?

*Developing Psychic
Communication with Your Pet*

RICHARD WEBSTER

What is your pet thinking?

Cats who predict earthquakes, dogs who improve marriages, and horses who can add and subtract—animals have long been known to possess amazing talents. Now you can experience for yourself the innate psychic abilities of your pet with *Is Your Pet Psychic?*

Learn to exchange ideas with your pet that will enhance your relationship in many ways. Transmit and receive thoughts when you're at a distance, help lost pets find their way home, even communicate with pets who are deceased.

Whether your animal walks, flies, or swims, it is possible to establish a psychic bond and a more meaningful relationship. This book is full of instructions, as well as true case studies from past and present.

0-7387-0193-9
288 pp., 5³⁄₁₆ x 8 $12.95

Also available in Spanish

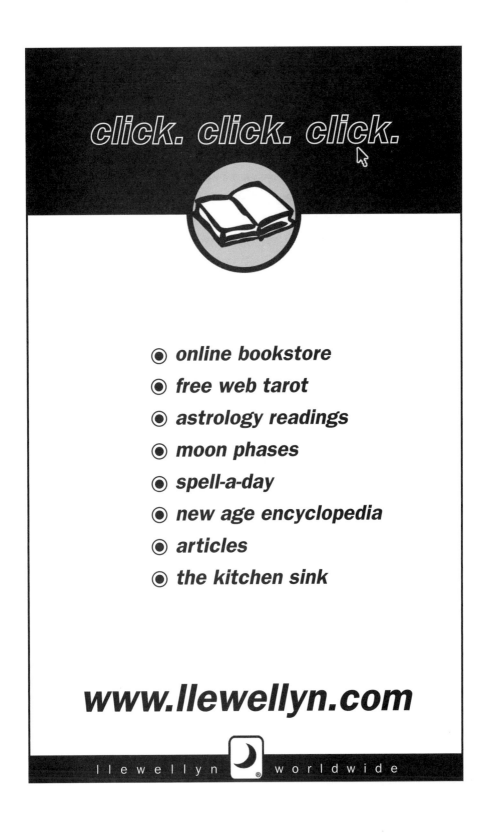

To Write to the Author

If you wish to contact the author or would like more information about this book, please write to the author in care of Llewellyn Worldwide and we will forward your request. Both the author and publisher appreciate hearing from you and learning of your enjoyment of this book and how it has helped you. Llewellyn Worldwide cannot guarantee that every letter written to the author can be answered, but all will be forwarded. Please write to:

Dr. Monica Diedrich
℅ Llewellyn Worldwide
P.O. Box 64383, Dept. 0-7387-0629-9
St. Paul, MN 55164-0383, U.S.A.

Please enclose a self-addressed stamped envelope for reply,
or $1.00 to cover costs. If outside U.S.A., enclose
international postal reply coupon.

Many of Llewellyn's authors have websites with additional information and resources. For more information, please visit our website:

HTTP://WWW.LLEWELLYN.COM